PitmanScript
Skill Book 2
(Speed Development)

PitmanScript
Skill Book 2
(Speed Development)

100 Examination Speed Tests
selected by
Emily D. Smith
B.Sc.Econ. (Hons.), F.R.S.A.

PITMAN

PITMAN PUBLISHING LIMITED
128 Long Acre, London WC2E 9AN

Associated Companies
Pitman Publishing Pty Ltd, Melbourne
Pitman Publishing New Zealand Ltd, Wellington

© Pitman Publishing Limited 1970, 1975
Second Edition 1975
Reprinted 1978, 1979, 1981, 1985

Made and printed in Great Britain
by Antony Rowe Ltd., Chippenham

ISBN 0 273 00915 X

ACKNOWLEDGMENTS

The publishers acknowledge with sincere thanks the permission of the following Examining Bodies to use a selection of their Shorthand Speed Tests:

East Midland Educational Union

London Chamber of Commerce

Pitman Examinations Institute

Royal Society of Arts

Union of Lancashire and Cheshire Institutes

Welsh Joint Education Committee

Yorkshire Council for Further Education

CONTENTS

PREFACE

The hundred passages that have been used in this dictation book are all tests set by leading shorthand examination bodies. The tests are counted in tens, so that they may be dictated at any desired speed, and they have been placed in order of length, the first test containing only 121 words, and the hundredth test containing 550 words.

It is suggested that each test should be dictated more than once in order that facility in writing is gained. This is particularly desirable with the shorter passages. Writers will also derive much benefit from using the tests as facility drills. The most satisfactory way of doing this is for the writer to copy out a passage, leaving two blank lines below every line of PITMANSCRIPT, and afterwards to use these blank lines for further copying. In order to gain the ability to write for four or five minutes consecutively, it is useful to prepare sufficient material to cover this length of time, and then to write the whole of it without a break. If such practice is done regularly, the ability to write for long periods will soon be developed.

It is very important during this practice, as well as when writing from dictation, to write very lightly. The pen or pencil should be held lightly, not gripped tightly, and only the lightest pressure is required to write the forms satisfactorily — in fact, the lighter the better. A tight grip and a heavy pressure cause the hand to tire and are a real handicap to speed.

The characters should also be written fairly small, as a large and sprawling style is a waste of effort and paper. The pen or pencil should just skim the paper, racing along without physical effort.

It is important to avoid physical effort, because the real place for effort during PITMANSCRIPT writing is in the mind. The mind is kept occupied hearing and interpreting what is being said. If the material being written in PITMANSCRIPT is fully understood while it is being written, it is afterwards easy to read it back. Mistakes arise from lack of understanding, and notes should not be written with the mind thinking about all sorts of other things. There must be complete concentration on the task of writing so that when the dictation is finished the writer knows in considerable detail just what has been written. Transcription then becomes both simple and accurate.

If for any reason difficulty is experienced during transcription in reading a particular form, a useful trick is to ask: "What would I have written in that sentence if I had been writing the material?" This forces the writer to consider the sense, and the appropriate word can usually be supplied.

No transcription should be handed in for marking until it has been carefully checked, word for word, against the notes by the writer. It is quite common for failure to arise from mere carelessness — carelessness in missing out a line of the notes, carelessness in not thinking of the sense of what has been written, carelessness in spelling. It is always worth checking a transcript because when it has been completed and a second reading is undertaken, the writer is in a position to detect any slip much more easily than in the course of the first writing. An examiner or teacher is always sorry to have to deduct marks for errors caused, not through inability, but through carelessness.

So students must remember that care and attention to detail are part of the PITMANSCRIPT writer's assets.

A group of PITMANSCRIPT forms has been given at the head of each dictation passage. The student should write each form several times before attempting the passage. The teacher can usefully show derivative forms and kindred outlines. Familiarity makes for speedy writing, and rapid drill on separate forms helps to bring such familiarity.

Another point that must not be overlooked is that PITMANSCRIPT is an individual system, and the writer is free to write as much or as little of a word or group of words as seems necessary in the circumstances. If a long word occurs with frequency in the same passage the writer will naturally abbreviate it. In the same way, shortcuts will be found for words and expressions that often occur in the course of work in an office. PITMANSCRIPT is a flexible system, and the writer must make it work in his service if he is to get the maximum benefit from it. Further, it is always better to write something than nothing. If a gap is left in the notes the chances that memory will supply the word are slim, but even badly written forms can often be read back accurately. It is wiser, therefore, to write a faulty form than to write nothing at all. The proper use of the rules of the system will, however, generally prevent faulty forms from being written.

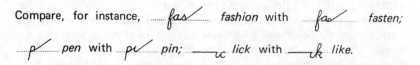

Compare, for instance, _____ fashion with _____ fasten; _____ pen with _____ pin; _____ lick with _____ like.

All the forms which appear in the PITMANSCRIPT *Word List* must be known so well that they can be written automatically, completely without hesitation, and the writer's general reading should be extensive in order to enlarge vocabulary and improve spelling ability. A misspelling can mar an otherwise perfect letter or document.

Points to remember are:

1. Write lightly and hold the pen or pencil lightly;
2. Write a neat and compact style; do not sprawl;
3. An imperfect form is better than a gap;
4. Follow with understanding what is being dictated;
5. Use commonsense when transcribing;
6. Always check the transcript before handing it in for marking;
7. Take each passage from dictation more than once, first drilling the forms given at its head;
8. Practise the passages as facility drills;
9. Know by heart the most common PITMANSCRIPT forms;
10. Improve vocabulary and spelling by extensive reading;
11. Long words can usually be written as far as the accented syllable only, e.g. *particular, individual*;
12. In links lightly-sounded or repeated consonants may be omitted, e.g. mus(t)be, nx(t) month, as(s)oon.

FURTHER NOTES

As has been stressed, PITMANSCRIPT is a flexible system. When writers feel that they possess a good command of the basic principles they are at liberty, if they wish, to adopt individual devices to meet their own special needs. This is particularly true in business life where a writer may find that he is constantly taking down the same words or expressions, and that an abbreviating device would be useful and time-saving.

There are various little ways in which fractions of seconds can be gained. For instance, *w* is one of the longer letters of the alphabet, and the word *we*, written ⏦, is very common. Time can therefore be saved when two *w*'s occur in succession by writing only a little upward tick for the first *w*, as:

⏦ = we will, ⏦ = we were, ⏦ = we want.

m is another rather complicated letter of the alphabet, and when two *m*'s occur in succession a fraction of a second can be saved by writing a little downward tick for the first *m*, close to the second one, as:

⏦ = memory, ⏦ = member.

With regard to the omission of vowels, it must be remembered that (except for *e* before *x*) all initial vowels are shown. The final vowel is represented by the little dash (⏦ = sunny) and is so quickly written that there is no justification for omitting it. It is, therefore, the medial vowel that lends itself to omission, and vowels can often be left out *in words of more than one syllable.*

As mentioned, longer words can usually be abbreviated by writing as far as the accented syllable, e.g. *partic*ular, *perpendic*ular, *pecu*liar, *famil*iar, *abbrev*iation.

Another form of abbreviation is that seen in advertisements: *adv* = advertisement, *mod* = modern, *conv* = convenience, *sal* = salary. When looking at advertisements we read such abbreviations without hesitation.

The suggestions for links made in the *Basic Text* and in *Skill Book 1* should be thoroughly mastered and applied.

Very lightly sounded consonants can be omitted at the end of words, such as *xpc* for *expect,* *pc* for *respect,* and in the same way lightly sounded or repeated consonants may be omitted in links. Examples are: *m̅ₐᵥ.* = *must have,* *xy* = *next year,* in which the final *t* of the first word is lightly sounded; and *ao⁄f* ...... *as soon as possible,* in which a repeated *s* is omitted, and *u̲̲p̲* = *your reply* in which a repeated *r* is omitted.

E.D.S.

1

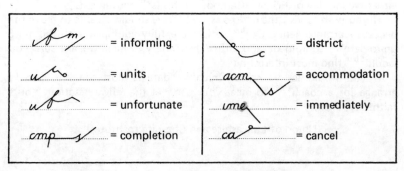

Dear Sirs, Thank-you-for-your-letter informing-us that[10] you-will-not-be able-to supply for another six[20] weeks-the new steel sink units for-the houses being[30] built on-the North Estate. This is very unfortunate as[40] it means we shall be held up with our completion[50] dates for the houses.

These houses are required for families[60] who will be moving to this district from another part[70] of the country and unless we finish building on time[80] they will have to seek other accommodation. Because of this[90] we have decided to obtain the sink units from another[100] firm who can supply them immediately. We shall have no[110] choice but to cancel the order with your firm. Yours[120] faithfully, (121)

(Union of Lancashire and Cheshire Institutes)

2

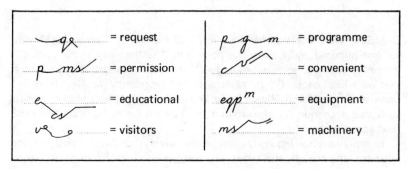

Dear Sir, Your request for permission to bring a party[10] of fifty students on an educational visit to our factory[20] next week has been handed to me for attention. As[30] you know we are always glad to receive visitors, and[40] we should be pleased to arrange a suitable programme. We[50] would suggest either Wednesday or Friday afternoon, if this is[60] convenient.

If you wish to visit the offices as well,[70] we should be able to make the necessary arrangements. Our[80] offices are fully equipped with the most up-to-date[90] equipment and office machinery, which we are sure you would[100] find most interesting.

If you would let us know which[110] date is most suitable, I could arrange for a coach[120] to meet your party at the railway station. Yours faithfully, (130)

(Union of Lancashire and Cheshire Institutes)

3

ℓ___m = settlement	= drilling
omu = omitted	m = mentioned
= deduct	c = reconditioned
p = representative	ap x = approximately

Dear Sirs, We thank you for your letter of yesterday,[10] enclosing cheque for one hundred and twenty-five pounds in[20] settlement of your account. You have omitted, however, to deduct[30] the sum of twenty pounds which you were kind enough[40] to advance to our representative when he called upon you[50] in March. Please let us know whether you would like[60] us to send you a cheque for the amount or[70] pass it on to your credit in the next account.[80]

In reply to your inquiry regarding the prices of drilling[90] machines for your training school, the types you mentioned range[100] from ninety to one hundred and fifty pounds. From time[110] to time we are able to supply reconditioned machines at[120] approximately half their original price.

If you are interested in[130] purchasing any machine either new or second hand we shall[140] be pleased to let you have further details. Yours faithfully, (150)

(Union of Lancashire and Cheshire Institutes)

4

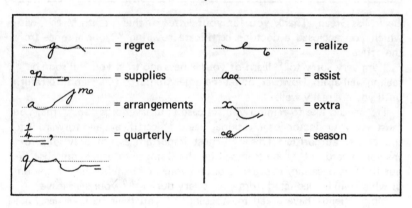

= regret	= realize
= supplies	= assist
= arrangements	= extra
= quarterly	= season

Dear Sir, It has been á matter of regret to[10] us that, during the past few years, we have had[20] to reduce supplies of our goods to you and others[30] in the trade who have been dealing with us for[40] so many years.

It gives us very much pleasure, therefore,[50] to tell you that arrangements have now been made for[60] an increase of fifteen per cent in your quarterly supply[70] of our special lines. This is, of course, in addition[80] to any of the increases we have been able to[90] make in the past. It will take effect from the[100] beginning of the next quarter. You will realize that this[110] increase is not nearly as much as we would like[120] it to be, but we hope that it will assist[130] you in meeting the extra demands that are bound to[140] be made upon you during the coming season. Yours faithfully, (150)

(Pitman Examinations Institute)

5

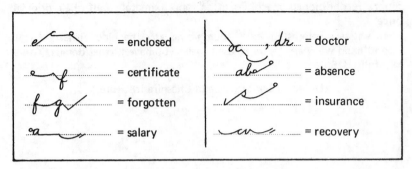

℮⌒° = enclosed	⟩𝒹𝓇 = doctor
℮⌒ƒ = certificate	𝒶ℓ𝒷 = absence
ƒ𝑔𝓋 = forgotten	⟋ = insurance
ℯ𝑎 = salary	⌣𝒸𝓋 = recovery

Dear Miss Green, Thank you for your letter of the[10] tenth March, with which you enclosed a doctor's certificate covering[20] your absence from the office.

I am very sorry to[30] learn of your illness and trust you will soon be[40] feeling well again. However, do let me urge you not[50] to attempt to return until you are really well.

I[60] should like to remind you, in case you have forgotten,[70] that you must ask your doctor for a National Health[80] certificate and forward it to the proper authorities. This is[90] most important as not only will your Insurance card not[100] be stamped by the Company during your absence, but it[110] is necessary in order to obtain your sick benefit, the[120] amount of which will be deducted from your salary during[130] your sick leave.

Your friends have asked me to send[140] you their best wishes for a speedy recovery. Yours sincerely, (150)

(Royal Society of Arts)

6

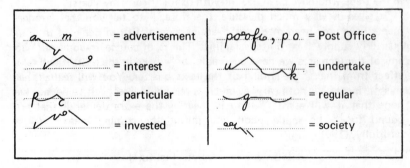

𝑎 𝓂 = advertisement	𝓅𝑜𝑜𝒻𝑜, 𝑝 𝑜 = Post Office
ℯ = interest	𝓊 𝓀 = undertake
𝓇 = particular	𝑔 = regular
⟋ = invested	ℯ𝑒𝓎 = society

Dear Sir, I have seen your advertisement in the local[10] paper in which you invite people who are interested in[20] saving money to write to you for details of your[30] schemes.

In the particular scheme which you mention in the[40] advertisement you offer a rate of five per cent on[50] sums invested with you above four hundred pounds. Personally, I[60] am not interested in this offer as I have put[70] my small capital into the Post Office Savings Bank. What[80] I would very much like to know, however, is whether[90] you have a plan under which I can receive a[100] higher rate of interest than five per cent if I[110] undertake to save a regular monthly sum. I know that[120] most of the big Building Societies offer a special higher[130] rate of interest on regular savings, and I shall be[140] glad to know whether your Society does this. Yours faithfully, (150)

(Pitman Examinations Institute)

7

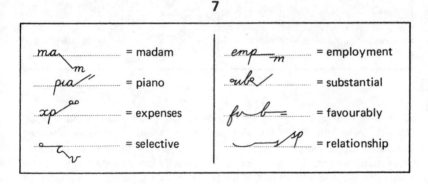

= madam		= employment
= piano		= substantial
= expenses		= favourably
= selective		= relationship

Dear Madam, We enclose details of charges for piano tuning[10] which will apply from 1st October, 1969.[20]

The last time we raised our charges was in[30] September, 1965. Since that date our[40] running expenses have increased, and in most cases increased very[50] considerably. In addition there has been imposed the Selective Employment[60] Tax, with which you are probably familiar.

We feel sure[70] you will understand that the present increases in our charges[80] must be substantial, as we have not, like so many[90] other firms, advanced our charges year by year. We feel,[100] too, that our prices compare very favourably with other service[110] charges, where skilled workers have to be employed.

We hope[120] that the happy relationship which has always existed between us[130] will continue, and that we shall have the pleasure of[140] keeping your piano in perfect working order for many years[150] to come. Yours faithfully, (154)

(Yorkshire Council for Further Education)

8

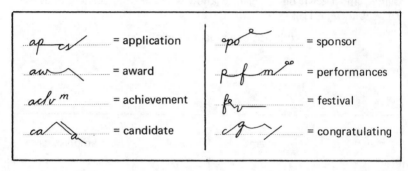

ap—cv	= application	*opo*	= sponsor
auv	= award	*p—f—mv*	= performances
aclv m	= achievement	*fev*	= festival
ca	= candidate	*cgv*	= congratulating

Dear Miss Young, I am very sorry indeed that your[10] application for an Award under the Council's Annual Youth Award[20] Scheme was not successful but I must tell you how[30] impressed the Committee was with your achievement. The selection of[40] the winning candidate was a most difficult task and I[50] should like you to know that a similar application from[60] you or your sponsor next year might well be successful.[70]

The performances of all candidates competing for the Award were[80] most pleasing and I hope sincerely that you will attend[90] the Youth Festival to be held on Saturday, 4th May.[100] I feel sure you would like to join the youth[110] of the area in congratulating the winner, and I am,[120] therefore, enclosing a special Privilege Ticket, so that you may[130] take your place on the platform with the other Highly[140] Commended candidates.

The Committee looks forward to meeting both you[150] and your parents on this very special occasion. Yours sincerely, (160)

(Royal Society of Arts)

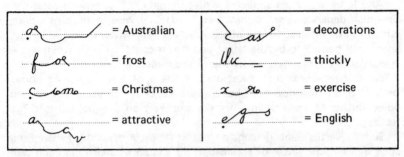

= Australian		= decorations	
= frost		= thickly	
= Christmas		= exercise	
= attractive		= English	

Dear Mary, I have been thinking of you enjoying the[10] lovely Australian sun.

Here the first days of December were[20] very cold. The north winds reached gale force and heavy[30] rain fell. Then came frost and the ice on the[40] roads was very dangerous. However, towards the middle of the[50] month the weather turned milder and we were able to[60] think about going out to do our Christmas shopping.

The[70] shop windows looked gay and attractive and inside there was[80] such a selection of goods it was difficult to make[90] a choice. Everyone seemed to have a great number of[100] parcels and the streets were crowded.

As the afternoons became[110] darker the decorations strung across the roads were lit up[120] and made the town look so pretty.

After Christmas it[130] turned cold again and snow fell thickly. The children got[140] out their sledges and took them to the hills outside[150] the town to enjoy the exercise and bracing air.

I[160] am looking forward to your visit here in August so[170] that you can enjoy our English sun. Love from Jane. (180)

(Pitman Examinations Institute)

10

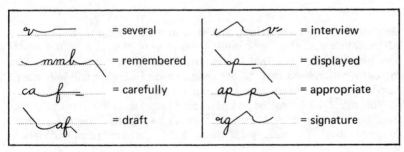

= several		= interview	
= remembered		= displayed	
= carefully		= appropriate	
= draft		= signature	

When applying for a post there are several points to[10] be remembered. Any letter which an applicant writes should be[20] composed carefully. So much depends upon it that it is[30] certainly wise to prepare a draft which can be altered[40] until it is satisfactory. The writer must realize that she[50] will be judged by the letter, and that it could[60] decide whether she is worthy of an interview or whether[70] she is quite unsuitable.

At any interview that takes place[80] the applicant may score points because of the neatness of[90] her appearance, or her pleasing manner and voice, but in[100] the first instance she must rely on the quality of[110] her letter.

Some advertisements demand a hand-written reply, but[120] if there is no such demand the letter of application[130] should be well typed and well displayed. Details should be[140] given of all previous experience and any appropriate certificates gained.[150] The times available for interview should be stated, and care[160] should be taken not to omit the date at the[170] beginning of the letter, or the signature at the end. (180)

(Yorkshire Council for Further Education)

11

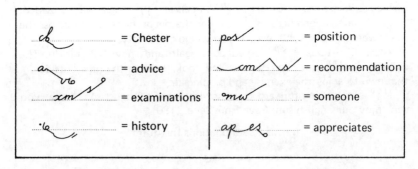

✍	= Chester	✍	= position
✍	= advice	✍	= recommendation
✍	= examinations	✍	= someone
✍	= history	✍	= appreciates

Dear Mr. Chester, I am writing this letter to thank[10] you for the help and advice which you gave me[20] while I was in your class at school. I am[30] very pleased to tell you that I have now heard[40] that I was successful in my examinations and that I[50] obtained a Credit in English and in History. I am[60] sure I owe this success to your patience.

You will[70] be interested to know that I have had an interview[80] at the local Bank, and I think I shall be[90] offered a position there as a clerk. However, it is[100] necessary for me to have a letter of recommendation

8

from[110] someone who knows me well. I shall be grateful, therefore,[120] if you will write a letter that I can take[130] with me to the Bank when I go for a[140] second interview next week.

My father has asked me to[150] say that he appreciates all that you have done to[160] help me and the other boys in your classes. I[170] shall let you know how I get on. Yours sincerely, (180)

(Pitman Examinations Institute)

12

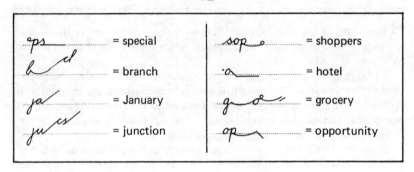

	= special		= shoppers
	= branch		= hotel
	= January		= grocery
	= junction		= opportunity

Dear Sir or Madam, We wish to draw your special[10] attention to the fact that a new branch of our[20] Stores will be opened in your district on the first[30] of January next.

This new Store is situated at the[40] junction of the High Street and Bridge Street, and is[50] on three floors. Everything will be provided for the convenience[60] of shoppers. On the top floor there will be two[70] cafés. One will offer food and service of a very[80] high quality, equal to the best hotel in the town.[90] The other will be a Self-Service Coffee Shop where[100] good food can be obtained quickly. There will also be[110] a Self-Service Grocery Department. Here we shall offer the[120] best goods at the lowest possible prices.

Another important addition[130] to the Store will be a pram-park, where two[140] ladies with the title of Nanny will be able to[150] keep an eye on the babies whilst their mothers are[160] shopping.

We hope that you will take an early opportunity[170] to call at our very fine new premises. Yours faithfully, (180)

(Pitman Examinations Institute)

13

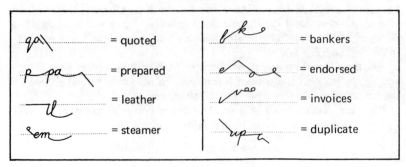 = light		= radiant
= important		= dark
= warm		= provide
= energy		= human

We need light to see with, but light is even[10] more important to us because it keeps the world warm,[20] and because without it we would have no food to[30] eat.

Without light from the sun the world would soon[40] freeze and be too cold for us to live in.[50] Sunlight is energy which warms up any matter it strikes.[60] We call the energy radiant heat when we feel its[70] warmth on our bodies and we call it light when[80] we see it with our eyes. The sun sends us[90] a great deal of both heat and light.

Even if[100] the world were warm enough we would have no food[110] without light. No green plants could live on an earth[120] that was completely dark. Green plants need light in order[130] to make their food and to get the energy with[140] which to grow. If there were no green plants there[150] would be no plant-eating animals. These in turn provide[160] food for the meat-eating animals. Without either green plants[170] or animals there would be no food for human beings. (180)

(Royal Society of Arts)

14

= quoted		= bankers
= prepared		= endorsed
= leather		= invoices
= steamer		= duplicate

Dear Sir, I thank you for the samples of brief[10] cases which were received on the 2nd March.

They were[20] of high quality and, at the price quoted, my company[30] is prepared to give you an order for six dozen[40] in brown leather and six dozen in black.

The order[50] must be shipped by fast steamer, freight paid, not later[60] than the 3rd April, insured against all risks, with claims[70] payable in London.

On our part we shall set up[80] a letter of credit in your favour through your bankers.[90] This will be paid against a draft presented with a[100] full set of bills of lading, endorsed in favour of[110] your bank, packing list and invoices in duplicate.

Provided the[120] quality of the delivered goods is up to that of[130] the samples I can say, with confidence, that my company[140] will be interested in further business with your firm, not[150] only in respect of brief cases, but in respect of[160] the whole range of your leather goods.

Finally let me[170] thank you for your attention in this matter. Yours faithfully, (180)

(Royal Society of Arts)

15

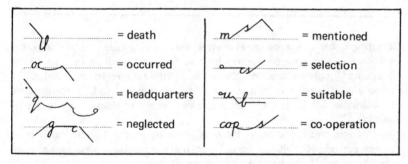

	= death		= mentioned
	= occurred		= selection
	= headquarters		= suitable
	= neglected		= co-operation

Dear Sir or Madam, It is with the deepest regret[10] that we have to inform you of the sudden death,[20] which occurred last Monday evening the 29th March, of[30] our representative who usually calls on you.

For the time[40] being we are looking after you direct from our headquarters,[50] so that you will not be neglected in the absence[60] of our representative's personal calls. We need hardly say that[70] visits to you will be resumed as soon as possible,[80] and we shall announce the name of our new representative[90] in your area as soon as we are in a[100] position to do so.

For this period we are pleased[110] to be able to offer you the goods mentioned in[120] detail overleaf. We hope this selection will be acceptable to[130] you, but if there is any item you do not[140] wish to include in the delivery, will you please make[150] a suitable note on the back of this letter and[160] return the letter to us as soon as possible.

May[170] we thank you in advance for your co-operation. Yours truly, (180)

(Pitman Examinations Institute)

16

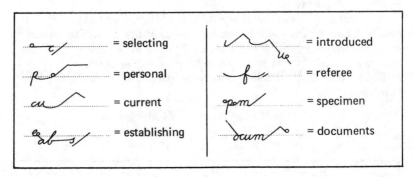

= selecting	= introduced
= personal	= referee
= current	= specimen
= establishing	= documents

Selecting a bank is a personal matter and, having taken[10] this step, the customer will go to a convenient branch[20] of that bank and say he wishes to open a[30] current account. Since this is the first step in establishing[40] a friendly relationship, it is usual for a new customer[50] to be introduced to the Manager, for he is the[60] man whose advice and help may one day be needed.[70]

A banker must ensure, as far as is possible, that[80] the customer is an honest person. He will be asked[90] to name a referee unless he has been introduced to[100] the bank by an existing customer.

When opening an account,[110] one of the first important steps is to give a[120] specimen signature. All future cheques that a customer signs will[130] be compared with this signature so it is important that[140] a signature remains constant. One should get into the habit[150] of signing letters, cheques and documents in the same way.[160] If the customer decides to change his signature, he should[170] inform the bank of this and provide a new specimen. (180)

(Yorkshire Council for Further Education)

12

17

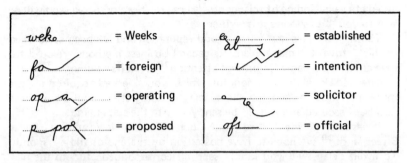

weke = Weeks	= established
= foreign	= intention
= operating	= solicitor
= proposed	= official

Dear Mr. Weeks, I am sorry to have to inform[10] you that I have now heard from the Authorities stating[20] that they cannot allow your claim for additional foreign currency.[30] I am enclosing a copy of the letter I have[40] received so that you can see for yourself the reasons[50] put forward.

You will observe that much importance is placed[60] upon the point that you have not at present any[70] business operating overseas. They stress that, although you state that[80] the purpose of your proposed tour is to ascertain whether[90] branches of your business could be established in various countries[100] overseas, the fact is that no such branches have been[110] established in the past and that there is no clear[120] evidence of any intention on your part to extend your[130] interests in this way.

In the circumstances I am obliged,[140] as your Solicitor, to suggest that you put off your[150] tour for the present. If you are not willing to[160] do this I make the alternative suggestion that you do[170] what you can on the basic official allowance. Yours faithfully, (180)

(Pitman Examinations Institute)

18

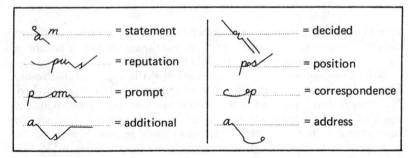

= statement	= decided
= reputation	= position
= prompt	= correspondence
= additional	= address

Dear Sirs, We have to inform you that the statement[10] for which you asked at the beginning of this month[20] has now been prepared, and will be sent to you[30] as soon as it is verified.

The firm in question[40] has a good reputation and has been established in this[50] town for many years. Its general business methods are up[60]-to-date and it has a name for prompt attention[70] in all its dealings.

The additional information for which you[80] asked required a little more investigation, and the slight delay[90] is regretted. Full details have now been secured and will[100] be sent you with the statement.

It has been decided[110] to remove our offices to New Buildings, Baker Street, and[120] we hope to have possession by the end of the[130] month. To avoid delay, will you kindly send all correspondence[140] to the new address after the end of the present[150] month.

With reference to your half-yearly account, it will[160] be in order to leave settlement until our representative calls[170] to see you again in four weeks' time. Yours faithfully, (180)

(Pitman Examinations Institute)

19

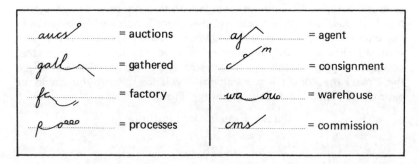

aucs	= auctions	_ay_	= agent
gall	= gathered	_c/m_	= consignment
_fa_	= factory	_wa ou_	= warehouse
_p_	= processes	_cms_	= commission

Most of the tea imported into the United Kingdom is[10] grown in India and Ceylon. Rather more than half the[20] tea supplied to Britain is bought in bulk at public[30] auctions which are held in London.

After being gathered on[40] the plantation, the leaf goes to the factory where it[50] passes through a number of processes before being packed. The[60] tea is then dispatched to the London agent of the[70] plantation. The agent of the tea estate will instruct a[80] selling broker to include the consignment in the next sales.[90] He will usually instruct him to get the best price[100] he can, though sometimes a price may be given to[110] him below which he must not sell. The selling brokers[120] inspect the packages in the warehouse, draw and test samples[130] and then compile catalogues.

Purchases at the sales are made[140] by buying brokers who normally buy to resell to blenders[150] and merchants on a commission basis.

Although there is nothing[160] in the rules of the market to prevent anyone bidding[170] at the auctions, in practice a broker is usually employed. (180)

(Royal Society of Arts)

20

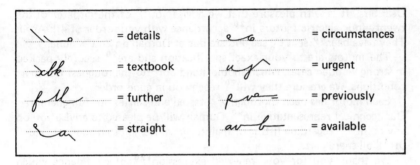

= details		= circumstances
= textbook		= urgent
= further		= previously
= straight		= available

Dear Mr. Brown, Thank you for your letter of yesterday[10] and for your order. Since we sent you details of[20] the new textbook "Preparation of Simple Accounts" there has been[30] a most unexpected demand from Colleges of Further Education throughout[40] the country. As a result, the book is out of[50] print at the moment.

Naturally, we are having the book[60] reprinted straight away, and hope to receive copies in two[70] weeks' time. In the circumstances, it is urgent for you[80] to let me know whether you are willing to wait[90] for delivery of the new textbook or whether you would[100] prefer us to send you a supply of the book[110] you were using previously. We have ample stocks of the[120] latter, and can send the copies by return of post,[130] if required.

We are happy to inform you that the[140] other books listed in your order are all available and[150] are being dispatched to you today. You will notice that[160] we have changed the binding of some of the books,[170] and shall be interested to have your opinion. Yours sincerely, (180)

(Pitman Examinations Institute)

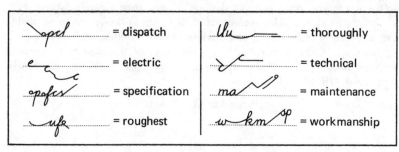

= dispatch	= thoroughly
= electric	= technical
= specification	= maintenance
= roughest	= workmanship

Dear Sirs, It is with pleasure that we advise you[10] of the dispatch of the twenty-four electric motors in[20] accordance with your order of 4th April. They have been[30] sent by sea and are due at Durban on 2nd[40] June.

The motors are to your exact specification and are[50] securely packed in strong wooden cases, which should stand up[60] to the roughest transport conditions. We are sure they will[70] reach you in good order.

Each motor has been thoroughly[80] tested and carries our full guarantee. Our technical representative in[90] Durban will be pleased to advise you on any point[100] regarding fitting or maintenance. He holds an adequate stock of[110] all spare parts.

We thank you for your renewed expression[120] of confidence which this further order shows, and you may[130] be quite sure that the goods now on the way[140] are of the same high standard of workmanship and material[150] which you have previously received.

We enclose with this letter[160] details of other electrical machines and spares, some of which[170] we think you may need in the future. Yours faithfully, (180)

(Royal Society of Arts)

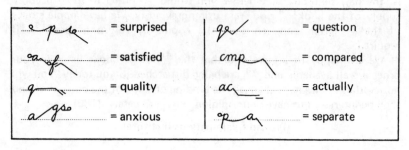

= surprised	= question
= satisfied	= compared
= quality	= actually
= anxious	= separate

Dear Sirs, We are both sorry and surprised to learn[10] that you are not satisfied with the quality of paper[20] supplied to you recently. This paper is in every way[30] up to the specification, and we cannot understand why you[40] are complaining. As you know, this particular paper is cheap,[50] and in our opinion it is very good value for[60] money.

We are, however, most anxious to please you because[70] you have been one of our customers for many years.[80] We therefore suggest that you return to us some sheets[90] of the paper in question, and we will have them[100] examined by our experts and compared very carefully with the[110] sample sent to you. If any difference can be found[120] between the sample and the paper actually sent, we shall,[130] of course, at once send you a fresh supply.

In[140] the meantime, we are sending you, under separate cover, some[150] samples of paper of a higher quality, as we think[160] you may be interested. The prices are marked on the[170] samples, and the paper can be supplied immediately. Yours faithfully, (180)

(Pitman Examinations Institute)

23

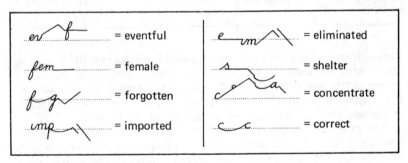

The past year has been an eventful one. Owing to[10] the shortage of female labour in the London area and[20] the huge increase in local rates we have had to[30] dispose of the factory there but the staff displaced have[40] not been forgotten.

The duty on imported paper has now[50] been eliminated and for the first time for more than[60] thirty years the industry has to face foreign competition without[70] the shelter of tariffs. There were two choices open to[80] us: we could fade out quietly from the scene or[90] we could develop and concentrate on those sectors of the[100] paper trade in which foreigners do not have the great[110] advantage of producing their own raw materials. We have chosen[120] the latter alternative and as we must have the correct[130] tools to do the job we are committed to heavy[140] expenditure on paper-making machinery, the benefit of which we[150] shall not reap for some time. We are engaged in[160] an expanding market and I have not the slightest doubt[170] that your company can look forward to a glowing future. (180)

(Royal Society of Arts)

24

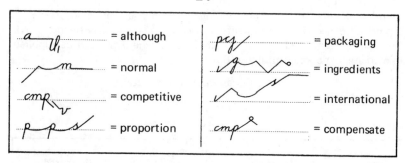

= although	= packaging
= normal	= ingredients
= competitive	= international
= proportion	= compensate

Although there has been some improvement our sales are still[10] running below what we deem to be normal but that[20] does not apply to our instant coffee which, in a[30] highly competitive market, is continuing to find increasing favour. I[40] should remind you, however, that our instant coffee sales are[50] a relatively small proportion of our turnover.

New processing machinery[60] has been installed and further changes are now being carried[70] out. Much attention is being given to the packaging of[80] our products and a new range has been introduced to[90] meet more precisely the needs of certain of our customers.[100]

The profitability of our business is affected both by volume[110] of sales and the price of our raw ingredients, particularly[120] coffee. The workings of the international coffee agreement have succeeded[130] in stabilizing prices but present indications are that coffee will[140] cost us more in the current year.

There are also[150] other factors at work and we continue to seek new[160] methods and to develop new products which could help to[170] compensate for any lower profit margins from our traditional lines. (180)

(Royal Society of Arts)

18

25

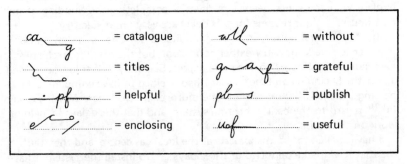

= catalogue	= without
= titles	= grateful
= helpful	= publish
= enclosing	= useful

Dear Sirs, I thank you for sending me the copy[10] of your catalogue and for marking the titles of the[20] books which you think would be most useful to me[30] in my studies. I have considered the matter very carefully,[40] and I now wish you to send to me one[50] copy of each of the seven books I have set[60] out below. I think these should be very helpful to[70] me, and enable me to pass my examination easily.

I[80] am enclosing a cheque for £2.80. This covers[90] the cost of the books at 30p each, plus[100] 10p each for postage. I hope to sit for[110] the examination in three months' time. As I am anxious[120] to begin my studies at the earliest possible moment, I[130] hope you will find it convenient to send the books[140] to me without delay.

Before I close this letter I[150] want to say how grateful I am for the help[160] you have given me. If you publish any new books[170] which might be useful, please send me details. Yours faithfully, (180)

(Pitman Examinations Institute)

26

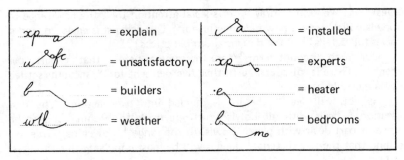

= explain	= installed
= unsatisfactory	= experts
= builders	= heater
= weather	= bedrooms

Dear Sir, I have received your letter of the 21st[10] October in which you explain why there has been[20] a delay in completing the building of my new house.[30] Your reasons for this delay are very unsatisfactory.

In the[40] first place, the other builders in this area have also[50] experienced the same bad weather conditions, but their building schemes[60] have not been affected to the same degree. Secondly, I[70] told you as long ago as the beginning of June[80] that I had decided to have complete central heating installed.[90] You cannot, therefore, claim that there was any delay in[100] regard to the central heating system, and that this delay[110] held up work on the house.

I have spoken to[120] the experts at the local gas centre, and they tell[130] me that it will take only two or three days[140] to install the system. I have decided to have the[150] main heater in the living room, with smaller ones in[160] the hall and in the bedrooms. This is a simple[170] matter, and should not cause any further delay. Yours faithfully, (180)

(Pitman Examinations Institute)

27

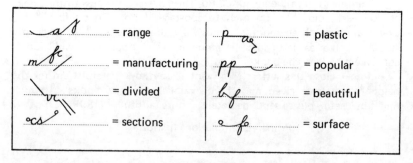

	= range		= plastic
	= manufacturing		= popular
	= divided		= beautiful
	= sections		= surface

Dear Sirs, We wish to draw your special attention to[10] the new range of bowls which we are now manufacturing.[20] Our new list is enclosed, and it gives full details[30] of the designs and retail prices.

Our trade discount terms[40] are the same as before; that is, thirty per cent.[50] There is, of course, a further five per cent for[60] accounts settled on a monthly basis.

As you will see,[70] the list is divided into two sections. The first section[80] deals with the bowls which are made from china, and[90] the second part deals with plastic bowls. In the range[100] of china bowls, we think that the size of ten[110] inches will be most popular with customers.

This bowl has[120] a depth of ten inches, and it is therefore ideal[130] for taking all kinds of bulbs.

Our plastic bowls are,[140] we think, the cheapest flower bowls on the market, yet[150] they are very beautiful. The reason is the special finish[160] we give to the surface of the plastic. Please let[170] us know your requirements as soon as possible. Yours faithfully, (180)

(Pitman Examinations Institute)

28

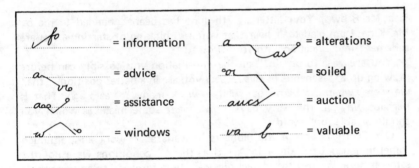

= information		= alterations
= advice		= soiled
= assistance		= auction
= windows		= valuable

Dear Sir, We thank you for the information given in[10] your last letter regarding premises for sale in your district.[20] For several years we have been anxious to open a[30] new branch in your town but we found it very[40] difficult to obtain suitable premises. The advice given in your[50] letter, however, has been of great assistance to us. We[60] wrote at once to the firm you named, with the[70] result that we have now agreed to purchase the shop[80] and the whole of the stock.

It will be necessary[90] for us to put in large new windows and to[100] make several alterations inside the building. Before this can be[110] done, however, we must dispose of the stock, as a[120] great deal of this is old or soiled. One of[130] our staff, who has examined the goods, suggests that the[140] best plan will be to sell them by auction and[150] this is what we intend to do very soon.

We[160] are greatly obliged to you for the interest you have[170] taken in this matter and also for your valuable help.[180] Yours truly, (182)

(Union of Lancashire and Cheshire Institutes)

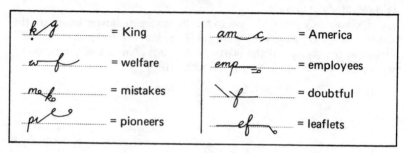

= King	= America
= welfare	= employees
= mistakes	= doubtful
= pioneers	= leaflets

Dear Mr. Brown, Your letter of 7th June has been[10] handed to me by Mr. King. I am glad to[20] hear that you are thinking of starting a welfare scheme[30] in connection with your firm.

You are wise to obtain[40] all the information you possibly can before drawing up a[50] scheme. In this respect you are in a better position[60] than we were, when we began our welfare work many[70] years ago. That is perhaps why, in the early days,[80] we made some mistakes which you should be able to[90] avoid.

Our firm was one of the pioneers in welfare[100] work and, although something had been done in America, the[110] conditions were not the same as here. We had to[120] feel our way, therefore, and to add one thing to[130] another as time went on. At first our employees did[140] not like the idea but now some of the keenest[150] supporters of the movement are to be found amongst those[160] who were doubtful.

I hope you will find the enclosed[170] leaflets helpful and I shall be pleased to give you[180] any further assistance. Yours truly, (185)

(Union of Lancashire and Cheshire Institutes)

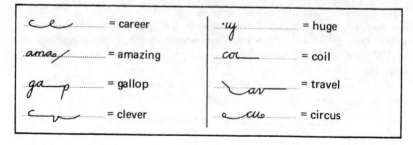

= career	= huge
= amazing	= coil
= gallop	= travel
= clever	= circus

Two hundred years ago a man returned from the Wars[10] and retired from his Army career. His love of horses[20] was great and so he bought several and trained them[30] to do amazing tricks. He could leap on them, stand[40] and climb on their backs even at a full gallop.[50] Then he had the idea that perhaps people would be[60] willing to pay to see his clever and beautiful animals.[70]

He found a farmer willing to rent him a large[80] field and employed small boys to run round the streets[90] telling people of the great display. Many people came and[100] the act was a great success. The only trouble was[110] that people at one end of the field could not[120] see what was happening at the other end. The next[130] day a huge coil of rope was borrowed and hung[140] round a circle of poles. By sitting round the circle[150] everyone could see what was happening.

Later other acts were[160] added to the show and the company began to travel[170] throughout this country and abroad. This was the beginning of[180] the travelling circus as we know it today. (188)

(Union of Lancashire and Cheshire Institutes)

31

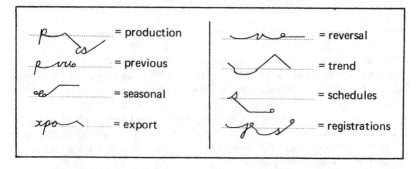

= production	= reversal
= previous	= trend
= seasonal	= schedules
= export	= registrations

The production of cars in this country fell by six[10] per cent during the month of May as compared with[20] the previous month. This figure takes into account both seasonal[30] factors and the differences in the number of working days[40] in the two periods. Production for export and the home[50] market both fell. The production in the four weeks of[60] May was thirteen per cent lower than in the same[70] period last year.

Despite this sharp drop, the production of[80] cars for the three months ending in May was ten[90] per cent higher than for the previous quarter. Production for[100] the home market rose whilst for exports it fell slightly.[110]

The reversal of the trend of rising production in May[120] is undoubtedly due to the revision of production schedules because[130] the number of registered cars has not been growing at[140] the same rate as production.

The industry, however, is confident[150] that the new regulations concerning hire purchase will increase new[160] registrations to a figure well above the low level of[170] the second half of last year. For the year as[180] a whole, however, registrations are unlikely to exceed those of[190] last year. Companies are trying to balance production with sales. (200)

(Royal Society of Arts)

32

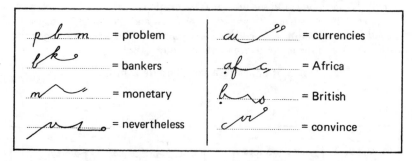

= problem		= currencies
= bankers		= Africa
= monetary		= British
= nevertheless		= convince

The basic problem being considered at the present time by[10] world bankers is to decide what place gold is to[20] have in the international monetary system of the future. It[30] has played a varying, but nevertheless essential, part for a[40] very long time and continues to do so.

In the[50] present monetary system, gold is the basis of all forms[60] of currencies. The system has worked well and this is[70] proved by the fact that international trade has been able[80] to grow at such a pace that it has doubled[90] in value every ten years.

There are, however, dangers in[100] the present system. One is that the supply of newly[110]-mined gold is growing rapidly in South Africa, but not[120] in the rest of the world whilst at the same[130] time the world-wide demand for gold for industrial purposes[140] is continually increasing.

A further danger arises from the wide[150] use of the British pound and the American dollar as[160] reserve currencies. This is an essential part of the system[170] but it depends entirely upon the ability of the United[180] Kingdom and the United States to convince other nations that[190] the dollar and the pound are as valuable as gold. (200)

(Yorkshire Council for Further Education)

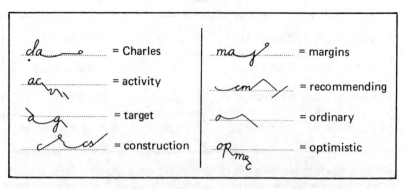

da	= Charles	ma	= margins
ac	= activity	cm	= recommending
	= target	o	= ordinary
	= construction	op	= optimistic

The second annual general meeting of Green and Sons, Limited,[10] was held on 17th March in London. Mr Charles Green,[20] the Chairman, presided, and the following is an extract from[30] his circulated statement:

Last year I stated that the building[40] industry was facing the highest level of activity in its[50] history and this has proved to be the case. The[60] Government's target of three hundred and fifty thousand houses was[70] exceeded and there was increased production in nearly all other[80] forms of construction.

During the year, gross profit margins were[90] generally at about the same level as last year, although[100] there was very keen competition in some directions. The net[110] profit before tax is six hundred thousand pounds, and we[120] are recommending a final dividend of fourteen per cent on[130] the ordinary stock.

There is still a very big unsatisfied[140] demand for houses, schools, hospitals and factories. The building industry[150] raised its output considerably last year, but, if the Government's[160] target for housing is to be realized, there will have[170] to be an increase in productivity.

Our Group's turnover since[180] the end of the financial year has been maintained and[190] I am optimistic regarding the future.

The report was adopted. (200)

(Union of Lancashire and Cheshire Institutes)

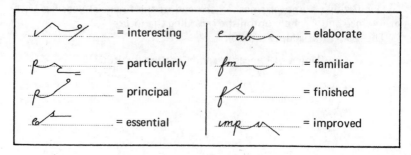 = publicity		= perfumed
= cosmetics		= economical
= necessity		= fashion
= priority		= expensive

With so much publicity given to cosmetics, and so many[10] new preparations appearing on the market, it is becoming more[20] and more difficult
to know which to choose and which[30] are the best value for money.

Necessity is the first[40] priority, but there are other factors which must
be taken[50] into consideration, such as effectiveness, ease of application,
and packaging.[60] There is no doubt that an unscented cream in a[70] plain
jar with no box will be cheaper than a[80] perfumed cream in an elegant jar
and an attractive box[90] but it does not necessarily follow that the cheapest cream[100] is the most economical. Although the price a woman is[110]
prepared to pay for her looks must largely depend upon[120] her budget,
the guiding factors are her age and individual[130] requirements.

An obvious economy is to buy the larger sizes[140] of skin care preparations, which do not go out of[150] fashion, and to buy the smaller sizes of
make-up.[160] Another point worth remembering is that the more expensive
the[170] cream, the smaller is the amount required for good results.[180]

Savings can also be made by buying the bargain packs[190] which are on
sale at certain times of the year. (200)

(Yorkshire Council for Further Education)

34

= interesting		= elaborate
= particularly		= familiar
= principal		= finished
= essential		= improved

Dear John, Thank you very much for your interesting letter[10] which I received yesterday. I was particularly pleased to learn,[20] above all else, that you have been chosen by the[30] Principal to address the first-year students.

The only way[40] I can help you at all is to suggest that[50] you should use no more words than are absolutely essential[60] to convey your meaning. On such an occasion I would[70] strongly urge you not to elaborate. In particular do not[80] use long words or phrases where simple ones would do,[90] for you may find yourself boring your audience rather than[100] keeping their attention. Familiar words are more likely to be[110] readily understood than the unusual.

When you are drafting your[120] address leave ample space on your paper. Large sheets are[130] useful for this purpose, for you can fold them down[140] the middle and leave the left half blank for any[150] additions or alterations you may wish to make afterwards.

When[160] you have finished your draft it is advisable to put[170] it away for a day or two; you will then[180] be in a far better position to see where it[190] could be improved.

I hope to hear from you again[200] soon that your address has been quite successful. Yours sincerely, (210)

(Pitman Examinations Institute)

36

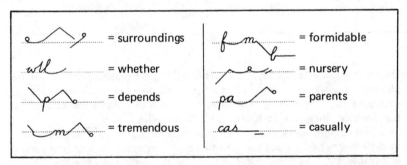

= surroundings		= formidable
= whether		= nursery
= depends		= parents
= tremendous		= casually

Most children will be returning to old familiar school surroundings[10] at the beginning of a new school year, but some[20] will be going to new schools, and a great many[30] will be going to school for the first time in[40] their lives. Whether or not they are going to make[50] a happy start and become part of the school depends[60] as much on parents as on teachers.

Attending school for[70] the very first time is a tremendous step in[80] a child's life. It is usually his first real break with[90] his mother, and with all the old familiar things and[100] faces at home. No matter how much he is looking[110] forward to it, or how brave a face he puts[120] on, school is something pretty formidable for one of such[130] tender years.

People in charge of nursery schools today realize[140] this and try to reduce the strangeness by suggesting that[150] parents take their children to see the inside of the[160] school at least once before the term begins. It is[170] also well worth while for parents to take their children[180] for walks past the school buildings as often as possible,[190] pointing it out casually as "his" or "her" school, so[200] that the child starts off with a sense of belonging. (210)

(Yorkshire Council for Further Education)

37

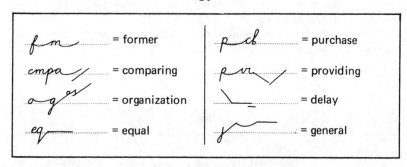

𝑓𝑚	= former	𝑝𝑐ℎ	= purchase
𝑐𝑚𝑝𝑎	= comparing	𝑝𝑣	= providing
𝑜𝑟𝑔𝑛	= organization		= delay
𝑒𝑞	= equal		= general

Dear Sir, I know that you, as a member of[10] this Building Society, will be pleased to learn that the[20] rate of interest on your ordinary shares is increased as[30] from today. The former rate of four pounds twelve and[40] a half has been increased to four pounds twenty-five.[50]

When comparing this rate of interest with rates paid by[60] organizations of different types, I must ask you to keep[70] in mind the fact that no tax is payable by[80] you, as the Building Society itself pays the tax. The[90] yield is therefore equal to over seven per cent in[100] cases where tax has to be paid.

It is hoped[110] by the Society that members will now increase the amounts[120] in their Share Accounts. It is also hoped that they[130] will recommend this form of investment to their friends. There[140] is at the present time a heavy demand for loans[150] for the purpose of house

28

purchase. The Society can meet[160] this demand only if large sums of money are invested,[170] thus providing the funds from which loans can be made.[180]

Interest is paid on a daily basis, and money can[190] be drawn out with the least possible delay. The Society's[200] assets now exceed fifty million pounds. Yours faithfully, General Manager (210)

(Pitman Examinations Institute)

38

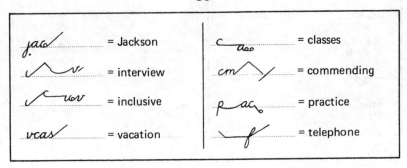

jac.	= Jackson	*c*	= classes
	= interview	*cm*	= commending
	= inclusive	*p ac*	= practice
vcas	= vacation		= telephone

Dear Miss Jackson, Referring to your interview with me yesterday,[10] I am now pleased to offer you a position with[20] this company upon the following terms.

Your hours of duty[30] will be from nine o'clock until five from Monday to[40] Friday inclusive. You will be allowed one hour for lunch,[50] and a quarter of an hour between ten-thirty and[60] eleven in the morning for a coffee.

During your first[70] two years with the company you will have two weeks'[80] paid vacation, apart from the usual Bank holiday weekends. Thereafter,[90] the period of leave will be three weeks.

You will[100] be employed in the advertisement section, and will be expected[110] to attend staff-training classes twice a week. The days[120] on which you will attend the classes will be decided[130] when you are actually with us.

We can offer you[140] a commencing salary of ten pounds a week, and this[150] will be subject to revision at the end of six[160] months. The practice of this company is to review salaries[170] twice a year, namely, in June and in December. Increases[180] are granted strictly according to merit.

If these terms are[190] agreeable to you, kindly telephone my secretary and confirm[200] that you will start work here on Monday next. Yours faithfully, (210)

(Pitman Examinations Institute)

39

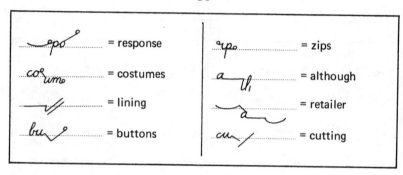

	= response		= zips
	= costumes		= although
	= lining		= retailer
	= buttons		= cutting

Dear Madam, In response to your request we now have[10] pleasure in sending you two books of sample materials. All[20] the cloth in the book marked A is suitable for[30] ladies' two-piece costumes, while in book B are samples[40] of materials for men's suits.

The cost of a lady's costume made in any of the materials numbers 1 to[60] 10 would be £15, while a model made up[70] in one of the remaining samples would be £[80]21. These prices include all necessary lining, buttons, zips, etc.[90] A booklet showing the various styles of costume we can[100] offer is enclosed.

A man's suit in any cloth from[110] 1 to 12 would cost £19, while in the[120] better materials 13 to 20 the price would be £[130]26.

Although we offer both ladies' and men's suits[140] in two grades, we can assure you that in both[150] grades the materials used are of very high quality. It[160] is possible to offer these very reasonable prices only because[170] we trade direct, thus cutting out the profit of the[180] retailer.

We shall be grateful if you will kindly return[190] the books of sample materials at your earliest convenience as[200] there is a very great demand for these. Yours faithfully, (210)

(Pitman Examinations Institute)

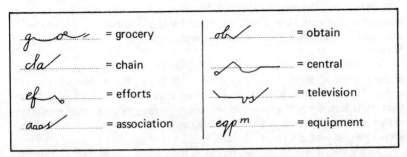

grocery symbol	= grocery	*obtain symbol*	= obtain
chain symbol	= chain	*central symbol*	= central
efforts symbol	= efforts	*television symbol*	= television
association symbol	= association	*equipment symbol*	= equipment

Dear Sirs, You will, of course, be aware of the[10] many changes that have taken place in the retail trade[20] of this country. The most important change has been in[30] the grocery business, and a large number of small firms[40] has been forced out of business by big chain stores.[50]

It is possible that your firm is facing this strong[60] competition, but we are certain we can help you in[70] your efforts to continue your business. The proof of this[80] claim is that we have this year helped no less[90] than five hundred grocers. We formed an association of grocers[100] who have undertaken to buy all their requirements from our[110] own central organization. In this way they obtain their stocks[120] at a low cost because our central organization can save[130] money through buying large quantities.

Members of the association not[140] only get their stocks at lower prices but they enjoy[150] other services. For example, we advertise widely in the national[160] newspapers and on television. We also assist in such matters[170] as insurance of shops and the provision of up-to-date[180] equipment.

Please let us know if you are interested[190] in being a member of our association. If so, we[200] shall send you full details of the scheme. Yours faithfully, (210)

(Pitman Examinations Institute)

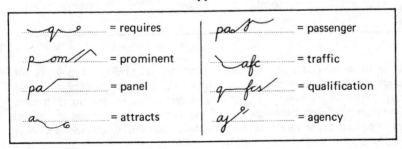

requires symbol	= requires	*passenger symbol*	= passenger
prominent symbol	= prominent	*traffic symbol*	= traffic
panel symbol	= panel	*qualification symbol*	= qualification
attracts symbol	= attracts	*agency symbol*	= agency

Dear Sir, As our company requires more staff, we shall[10] be glad if you will place an advertisement for us[20] in a prominent position in your evening newspaper. It should[30] be in the form of a panel, and should be[40] arranged in such a way that it attracts attention. The[50] advertisement is as follows:

"A well-known Air Line requires[60] staff for booking passenger flights and for making sales. Last[70] year this Air Line carried three and a half million[80] passengers. A very large staff of trained people is required[90] to deal with traffic on such a scale. We now[100] require staff at our London office and at various branch[110] offices to deal both with telephone enquiries and with personal[120] calls.

"Applications will be considered from men and women over[130] twenty-one years of age. An important qualification is the[140] ability to be polite and to be patient. It is[150] necessary to be able to talk to people from all[160] walks of life. Previous experience with an Air Line or[170] in a Travel Agency would be an asset.

"The salary[180] offered is seven hundred pounds per annum, increasing to eight[190] hundred pounds. Applications should be addressed to Box one hundred,[200] The Daily Post."

Please insert the above tomorrow. Yours faithfully, (210)

(Pitman Examinations Institute)

42

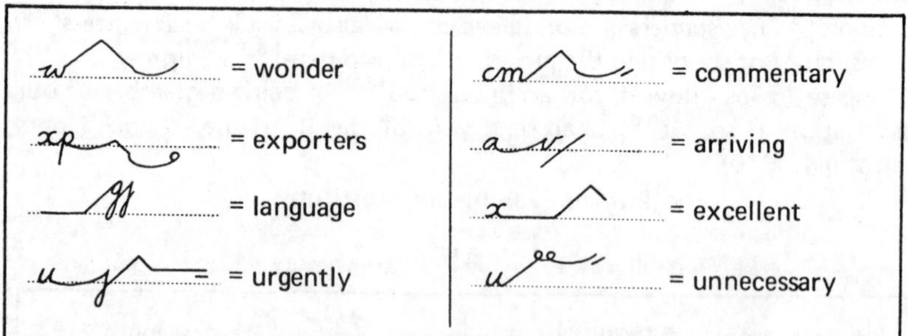

= wonder	= commentary
= exporters	= arriving
= language	= excellent
= urgently	= unnecessary

It is no wonder that many British exporters are under[10] heavy fire for poor selling efforts when they continue to[20] support the very old belief that there is no need[30] to use any language but English in their sales literature.[40] Some time ago one of my clients was expecting a[50] group of some half-dozen men from South America, all[60] of whom spoke English very well. He asked me, urgently,[70] to add a commentary in Spanish to a film he[80] wished to show his visitors. He also invited me to[90] be present, thinking I might be interested. I was.

Arriving[100] at the office I was introduced to the group who[110] did indeed speak excellent English, and in his little theatre[120] the film began. When the commentator started speaking in Spanish[130] the reaction of the visitors was audible. At the end[140] of the show they could hardly say enough about the[150] great courtesy of my client in taking such trouble to[160] show them a film in their own language. I believe[170] a most satisfactory contract resulted.

There seems little doubt that[180] remarks to the effect that it is unnecessary to sell[190] to a man in his own language, whether in literature[200] or in films, are but very feeble excuses for inaction.[210] There is every need for this rewarding form of courtesy. (220)

(Royal Society of Arts)

43

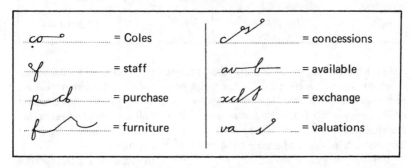

.ᴄᴏ.... = Coles		.ᴄ.... = concessions
.ᴣ.... = staff		.ᴀᴠ─ᵇ── = available
.ᴘ_ᴄʙ.... = purchase		.ᴢᴄ/ᴅ.... = exchange
.ᴊ.... = furniture		.ᴠᴀ_ᴊ.... = valuations

Dear Mr. Coles, It is some time since my staff[10] and I have had the pleasure of seeing you in[20] our Store. Why not give us a call, even if[30] you are not considering the purchase of furniture just now?[40]

We should like to remind you that as a valued[50] customer of ours, you are entitled to certain special concessions,[60] as follows:

(a) All goods available with no deposit and[70] forty weeks to pay.

(b) We will take your unwanted[80] furniture and carpets in part exchange towards the cost of[90] new purchases. We pay the highest prices for such items,[100] and make valuations in your home without obligation.

(c) An[110] extensive range of goods and services is always available to[120] you at attractive prices, and we offer generous hire purchase[130] terms.

(d) Estimates, measuring and fitting of carpets and underlays[140] are quite free to you, and all our carpets are[150] obtainable on the easiest of weekly terms.

(e) Above all[160] we give you value for money as our prices are[170] the most competitive in the trade, and everything we sell[180] is fully guaranteed.

As an incentive, a bone china tea[190] set will be presented to you if you place an[200] order to the value of twenty pounds or more within[210] four weeks of the date of this letter. Yours sincerely, (220)

(Royal Society of Arts)

44

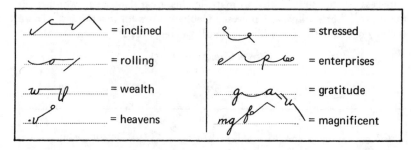

= inclined = stressed

= rolling = enterprises

= wealth = gratitude

= heavens = magnificent

I suppose all of us, as customers of oil companies,[10] are rather inclined to think of them as rolling in[20] wealth but when we are taking this view we are[30] sometimes a little apt to forget that this wealth does[40] not descend of its own accord from the heavens or[50] even well up from the earth, or, for that matter,[60] from the base of the sea, but that it results[70] from the extremely hard work of a very large number[80] of people.

If I may presume to say so, we[90] have achieved a very considerable success and it cannot be[100] stressed too often that it is on such commercial enterprises[110] as ours that the prosperity of this country does, in[120] a large measure, depend. Our contribution this year to the[130] balance of payments amounts to eighty million pounds.

I think[140] this is a matter for congratulation to the management, and[150] for gratitude on the part of the community. As for[160] gratitude what is it but a lively sense of future[170] favours? From what we have learned today I do not[180] think that even that form of gratitude is misplaced and[190] I have no doubt in my own mind that we[200] are greatly indebted both to the management and to all[210] engaged in this great task for a magnificent year's work. (220)

(Royal Society of Arts)

34

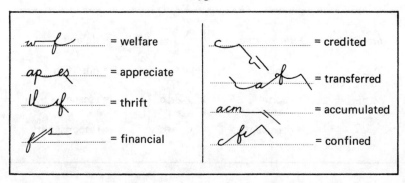

= welfare	= credited
= appreciate	= transferred
= thrift	= accumulated
= financial	= confined

Parents and others with the welfare of children at heart[10] will appreciate the advantages of opening a savings account for[20] them. A savings account not only encourages the habit of[30] thrift, but also enables children to establish an early connection[40] with the bank, which will stand them in good stead[50] in later life when they begin to assume responsibility for[60] their own financial affairs.

A home safe can be provided,[70] without charge, to help in the saving of coins and[80] notes. When this is full it is taken to the[90] bank and the contents credited to an interest-earning account.[100]

No one is too young to start a savings account,[110] but in the case of very young children it may[120] be preferable for the account to be opened in the[130] name of a parent. Later on, when the child is[140] old enough to sign his name on the account, it[150] can be transferred into the child's own name. When the[160] time comes that use can be made of a cheque[170] book, a current account, and all the other services offered[180] by the bank, a connection will already have been established[190] and a useful balance accumulated.

The advantages of a savings[200] account are not confined to the young, for there is[210] no easier way for persons of any age to put[220] aside regular sums of money. (225)

(Yorkshire Council for Further Education)

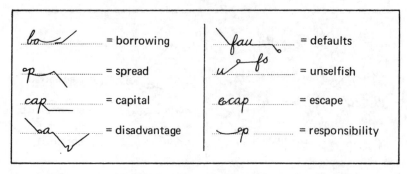

= borrowing			= defaults
= spread			= unselfish
= capital			= escape
= disadvantage			= responsibility

Few people who buy goods on hire purchase know the[10] amount they are really paying for borrowing money. Salesmen who[20] suggest the easy-payment method never tell us what is[30] the real rate of interest which we are paying to[40] the hire purchase company.

The buyer of a car might[50] be able to provide £200 towards a total[60] cost of £600. He borrows £400[70] from the company and is told that the interest rate[80] is ten per cent for each year. If the agreement[90] is for two years he will be paying a total[100] of £480, spread over twenty-four[110] monthly payments, beginning one month after the agreement is signed.[120]

Each payment includes some capital and the real rate of[130] interest is almost double the figure of ten per cent[140] quoted. A further disadvantage is that such interest payments cannot[150] be included in his income-tax return.

To bring the[160] interest payments within the scope of tax relief, a number[170] of schemes have been devised by which the agreement is[180] not really hire purchase, as the buyer is the legal[190] owner from the start, so that if he defaults he[200] has to be sued for debt. The purpose behind this[210] is not entirely unselfish. Because of recent changes in hire[220] purchase law, the finance companies cannot now escape responsibility[230] for the condition of a car bought in this way. (240)

(Yorkshire Council for Further Education)

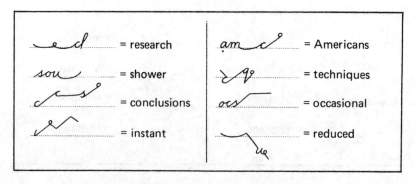

= research		= Americans
= shower		= techniques
= conclusions		= occasional
= instant		= reduced

Paper dresses are being made by several fashion firms but[10] as yet they are not selling very well. A consumer[20] research association recently organized tests on paper dresses already on[30] the market. It was found that they could be worn[40] three or four times before the dress tore and that[50] they stood up to a shower of rain quite well.[60] One of the conclusions reached, however, was that buying a[70] paper dress was not necessarily the cheapest way to instant[80] fashion. The dresses cost, on average, from 70p to[90] £1.20. As many dresses made from ordinary materials[100] can be bought for under £2, the paper dresses[110] were not considered to be a good bargain. Also, it[120] was pointed out that with the current length and style[130] of mini dresses, a girl did not have to buy[140] much material to make a dress of modern design.

At[150] the moment the Americans are ahead of Britain in the[160] new techniques involved in making paper suitable for dresses. One[170] large British fashion firm has already signed a three-year[180] agreement with an American producer to import the necessary basic[190] fabric.

Some designers have recently been successful with paper wedding[200] dresses and evening gowns, which are an obvious choice for[210] clothes that are for occasional wear only.

Much thought is[220] also being given to the idea of selling paper clothes[230] in packages so that the marketing costs can be reduced. (240)

(Yorkshire Council for Further Education)

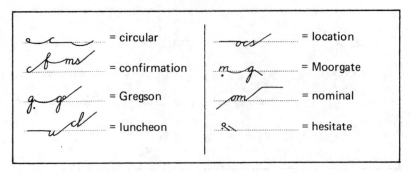

	= circular		= location
	= confirmation		= Moorgate
	= Gregson		= nominal
	= luncheon		= hesitate

Dear Sir, Since my circular dated sixteenth November, containing details[10] of our planned visits for the months of December, January,[20] and February, I have received confirmation that following the visit[30] of our members to Steel Rolling Mills, Ltd., on Monday,[40] eleventh December, Mr. P. Gregson, B.Sc., will attend[50] our Society's luncheon as our guest and after-luncheon speaker.[60] Mr. Gregson specializes in the teaching of mathematics and his[70] lecture should be of special interest to the majority of[80] members and to you in particular.

If you have already[90] applied for inclusion in the party to visit Steel Rolling Mills,[100] Ltd., and now desire also to attend the luncheon[110] and lecture, will you please complete the enclosed form of[120] application and return it without delay—an addressed envelope is[130] enclosed for this purpose.

As it is difficult to explain[140] the exact location of the firm to anyone who is[150] not familiar with this particular area, it has been arranged[160] that members who have made official application to visit the[170] Rolling Mills will be met in the entrance hall of[180] the Station Hotel, Moorgate, which is opposite the station, at[190] eight-thirty a.m. on Monday, eleventh December. A private[200] coach has been hired to transport our party to the[210] factory site and for this small luxury there will be[220] a nominal charge of 25p per person.

If[230] there should be any matter regarding our Society's future plans[240] on which you may wish me to comment, please do[250] not hesitate to ask my advice. Yours faithfully, Secretary **(259)**

(Royal Society of Arts)

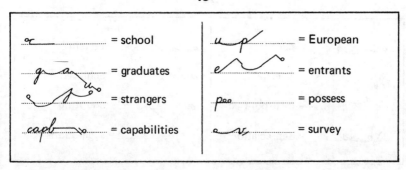

= school		= European
= graduates		= entrants
= strangers		= possess
= capabilities		= survey

The demand for business school graduates is likely to rise[10] sharply in the next few years as the new British[20] schools begin to produce their own trained manpower. These new[30] graduates will, however, for a long time remain strangers to[40] the normal business community. They will be men with a[50] different background and training from those of their colleagues.

A[60] survey has recently been carried out by the newly-formed[70] Business Graduates Association to find out just how different these[80] men are, and how their capabilities can be used within[90] industry. The survey has studied graduates from American and European[100] schools who are now employed by British firms.

A total[110] of one hundred and eighty graduates was considered, two-thirds[120] of them from American business schools, and the other one-[130] third from the European schools.

One interesting factor is the[140] age of the men involved, which falls, in most cases,[150] between twenty-six and thirty-five and not, as many[160] people would have supposed, under twenty-five. In other words,[170] entrants to business schools already possess some industrial experience.

A[180] table has been prepared showing the kind of salaries these[190] graduates commanded upon completing their courses, and as the lowest[200] figure is almost two thousand pounds, it is obvious that[210] the graduates have, on the whole, been given positions of[220] responsibility. The Association's survey shows that sixteen per cent of[230] those in the sample are now either chairmen or managing[240] directors of their companies, and eighteen per cent are directors[250] or partners.

This survey has gone a long way in[260] creating a more realistic attitude towards the new business schools. (270)

(Yorkshire Council for Further Education)

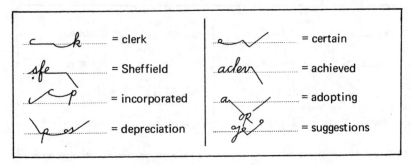

= clerk	= certain
= Sheffield	= achieved
= incorporated	= adopting
= depreciation	= suggestions

Dear Sirs, Our clerk has now completed his audit of[10] the accounts of your Sheffield branch and has delivered his[20] report to us. Before we incorporate the results submitted in[30] the combined statement, we should like to have your comments[40] on one or two points raised by our clerk. Although[50] they are not wholly related to the accounts, we think[60] that it is our duty to refer these matters to[70] you.

In the first place, the rate of depreciation allowed[80] on the machinery during the past year appears to us[90] to be insufficient, in view of the age of the[100] machines and the greater use to which they have been[110] put during the past twelve months. Few of the machines,[120] as you know, are less than five years old, and[130] as they have recently been used on day and night[140] shifts the wear and tear has been considerable. We suggest[150] that depreciation be increased by five per cent for the[160] year.

Secondly, our clerk has questioned the valuation of certain[170] items in the stocks of raw material and he has[180] been asked by the local manager to take this up[190] with you. The manager, himself, thinks that, in view of[200] the present position and future prospects of the market, the[210] values placed upon some of the items are well below[220] the figure at which they should appear.

We think that[230] a true valuation of the trading for the period would[240] be achieved by adopting the suggestions made but you, of[250] course, are in a better position to judge the facts[260] and we would not question your considered opinion on the[270] matter. Yours faithfully, (273)

(Union of Lancashire and Cheshire Institutes)

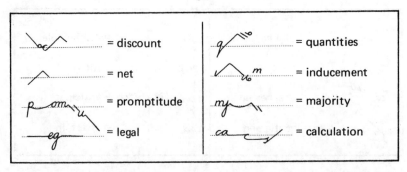

= discount		= quantities	
= net		= inducement	
= promptitude		= majority	
= legal		= calculation	

Trade discount is a deduction made by the seller before[10] charging the buyer with the price of the goods; the[20] net amount, after the deduction is made, is the sum[30] entered to the debit of the customer's account. The trade[40] discount is not affected by the promptitude with which the[50] amount owing is paid. If payment was not made and[60] legal action became necessary in order to recover the debt,[70] only the net amount, that is, the gross amount less[80] trade discount, could be actually sued for. Trade discount is[90] granted for several reasons.

Some manufacturers and wholesalers, when dealing[100] with retailers, may quote the retail selling price for an[110] article and make a deduction for trade discount, this representing the[120] retailer's gross profit on the deal. In some instances[130] a percentage deduction is made from every item sold to[140] the trade. Such a deduction really represents nothing in particular[150] as the net price is the only one expected by[160] the seller and, therefore, when fixing prices, they are settled[170] with full knowledge that, say, a five per cent deduction[180] will be made in all cases. The buyer is aware[190] of the fact, too, but it is referred to as[200] a trade discount.

Another example is the discount allowed when[210] large quantities are bought. This is an inducement to buy in[220] larger quantities and the manufacturer or merchant can usually afford[230] to give such an allowance as the larger quantities are[240] generally produced at less cost per unit than small quantities.[250]

With the majority of goods, however, no trade discount is[260] allowed. Where it is given the amounts vary considerably. Where[270] list prices are nominal and given only as a basis[280] for calculation of current prices by means of the discount,[290] the latter may be as much as fifty per cent. (300)

(London Chamber of Commerce)

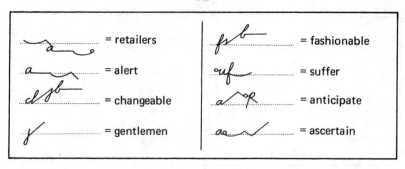

= retailers	= fashionable
= alert	= suffer
= changeable	= anticipate
= gentlemen	= ascertain

The retailer's first task is to cater for the needs[10] of his customers. If he wishes to make his business[20] a really successful one he must always be on the[30] alert so that he can note, at the earliest possible[40] moment, any change which may be taking place in the[50] character of his customers' requirements or of their tastes. Human[60] beings are very changeable on the whole and this is[70] particularly true in some special directions.

We may find in[80] a certain year that gentlemen are wearing shoes with pointed[90] toes more than any other type of footwear whereas in[100] the following year pointed shoes may be quite in disgrace.[110] A certain type of dress may be the fashionable one[120] for ladies this year but it will certainly not be[130] so in the following year. The retailer must watch these[140] changes very carefully because he will suffer a big loss[150] if an article goes out of fashion completely when he[160] is still carrying a large stock of that particular article.[170]

The retailer must therefore try to anticipate his customers' requirements.[180] It is difficult for him not to make a mistake[190] sometimes and particularly in businesses connected with clothes, footwear, etc.[200]

Most retailers require payment for their goods immediately; others are[210] prepared to allow customers to have goods for which it[220] is only necessary to pay after a time. In the[230] latter case we say that the retailer grants credit to[240] his customers. Before he allows customers to have goods on[250] credit he must know something concerning these people. He must[260] make it his business to ascertain whether they are likely[270] to prove trustworthy; if not he may have some difficulty[280] in getting paid for his goods and therefore lessening the[290] amount of money he has available for buying more goods. (300)

(London Chamber of Commerce)

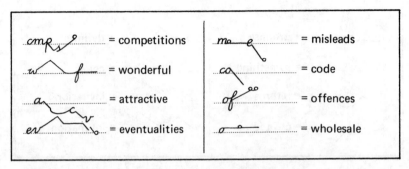

= competitions		= misleads
= wonderful		= code
= attractive		= offences
= eventualities		= wholesale

More and more companies are advertising their products by means[10] of competitions of various kinds. The competition is always very[20] simple so that almost anyone can attempt it while the[30] prize is always something very desirable like a wonderful holiday[40] and all expenses paid or a new car or something[50] equally attractive. Complaints from members of the public, however are[60] increasing.

The most frequent cause for complaint has been the[70] failure on the part of the companies promoting competition to[80] plan for all eventualities. Nobody is suggesting that there is[90] any intention to deceive the public but in one case[100] the total number of correct solutions submitted on the very[110] first day of the competition was larger than the number[120] of prizes. Despite this, however, the advertising programme was continued[130] as if successful entries still had a chance of a[140] prize.

Advertising which gives incorrect information or which misleads the[150] public is in fact very rare in this country. The[160] advertising industry has itself produced a code of conduct which[170] is strictly enforced. A few companies have been warned for[180] breaking the rules and they have been threatened that further[190] offences will be punished. A particularly widespread complaint is that[200] some advertising gives the impression of a price reduction by[210] comparing the selling price with one which is no longer[220] the usual price. On the other hand, some firms which[230] guarantee to refund the purchaser's money if the goods are[240] returned, try to play for time by replacing them with[250] other goods. Although some special offers still give cause for[260] complaint by reason of late delivery or delayed refund of[270] money the number of such cases is very small indeed.[280] All in all it is a matter of minor breaches[290] of the code of good conduct rather than wholesale misrepresentation. (300)

(Royal Society of Arts)

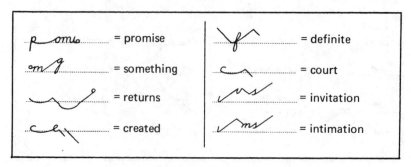

= promise		= definite
= something		= court
= returns		= invitation
= created		= intimation

An offer may consist of a promise to do or[10] pay something in return for either a promise by the[20] other party to do or pay something or an act[30] on the part of the other party. If Brown advertises[40] in a newspaper offering five pounds reward to anyone who[50] returns his lost dog, such advertisement is an offer. White[60] sees the advertisement, finds the dog and returns it to[70] Brown. White has thereby accepted the offer and a contract[80] has been created.

An offer may be made to a[90] definite person or it may be made to the world[100] at large, as in the advertisement for the lost dog.[110] An offer to the world must be accepted by a[120] definite person or persons. In a well-known case which[130] came before the Courts a firm advertised that one hundred[140] pounds would be paid to anyone contracting influenza after using[150] one of its smoke balls. A lady used the smoke[160] ball but she got influenza. The Court held that the[170] firm had made an offer and that the lady had[180] accepted it by using the ball and that in the[190] circumstances she could claim one hundred pounds.

If a shopkeeper[200] displays goods in his window with a ticket on them[210] denoting the price, his act is not an offer but[220] is merely an invitation to the public to make offers[230] to him; the price ticket is an intimation of the[240] terms on which the shopkeeper is prepared to accept them.[250] The customer cannot therefore insist on the shopkeeper selling him[260] the article, for the shopkeeper is absolutely free to accept[270] or reject just as he wishes.

A catalogue is only[280] an invitation to do business and the contents are only[290] statements of the kind of business done by the firm. (300)

(London Chamber of Commerce)

44

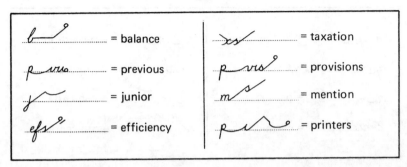

= balance	= taxation
= previous	= provisions
= junior	= mention
= efficiency	= printers

Dear Mr. Black, I have received your report on the[10] present position of our company and also the copy of[20] the final Balance Sheet and Profit and Loss Account. After[30] a thorough study of these papers, I wish to make[40] the following comments for your careful consideration. The most important[50] item is the satisfactory working of our company in nineteen[60] hundred and sixty-six as compared with our results in[70] previous years.

For example, we increased our sales by more[80] than fifteen per cent, and in addition our profit on[90] trading was almost twenty per cent greater than that for[100] the previous year. These are very important figures. I think,[110] indeed, that you should draw particular attention to them. The[120] fact is that they show that our study of the[130] use of labour has been successful. We have trained both[140] junior and senior managers to make the best possible use[150] of the information obtained by our efficiency experts. In this[160] way managers are able to organize the use of skilled[170] workers in order to bring about increased production.

Another important[180] matter to which attention must be drawn is that of[190] taxation. For the current year we shall be taxed under[200] the provisions of the Finance Act of the previous year.[210] I have worked out what we should have had to[220] pay in taxes if we were still operating under the[230] old tax arrangement. On the old basis we should have[240] had to pay £450,000 but[250] with the new taxation we shall have to pay[260] £760,000. There is only one other[270] item which needs special mention and that is the effect[280] of any new pay award. In my opinion this will[290] seriously affect our endeavour to hold prices at their present[300] level.

Please let me know the latest date for sending[310] the report and the accounts to the printers. Yours sincerely, (320)

(Pitman Examinations Institute)

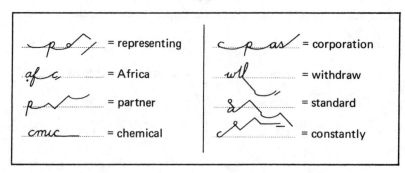

= representing		= corporation	
= Africa		= withdraw	
= partner		= standard	
= chemical		= constantly	

Dear Sirs, The purpose of this letter is to ask[10] you whether it is possible to enter into an agreement with your firm with a view to representing it in[30] South Africa.

I have an office in Cape Town, and[40] have contacts in all the major towns of this country.[50] I travel frequently to all parts of South Africa but[60] you need not fear any lack of attention to your[70] letters during my absences from Cape Town since my junior[80] partner is a very capable person.

Having lived for thirty[90] years in South Africa. I can assure you that I[100] have an excellent knowledge of all the requirements of the[110] import trade. For the last twenty years I have looked[120] after the interests of a well-known American firm, The[130] New York Chemical Corporation, and the President of that Corporation[140] will give you any information you may require. The reason[150] for the ending of my agency for the Corporation is[160] that they have recently entered into an agreement with another[170] important exporter of chemicals from the United States to share[180] certain overseas markets. Under the terms of this arrangement, The[190] New York Chemical Corporation have to withdraw from the South[200] African market.

With regard to my financial standing, I should[210] be pleased if you would refer to the Manager, The[220] Standard Bank, Main Street, Cape Town. If you do not[230] care to settle direct with customers abroad, I should be[240] willing to arrange for an English bank to make cash[250] payments in London on presentation of Bills of Lading.

Another[260] important service that I can render is the supply of[270] monthly reports on trading conditions in South Africa. My contacts[280] in the trade constantly keep me informed of all important[290] developments, and this information would be of great value in[300] enabling you to judge the future trend of trade.

Kindly[310] let me know if this proposal interests you. Yours faithfully, (320)

(Pitman Examinations Institute)

57

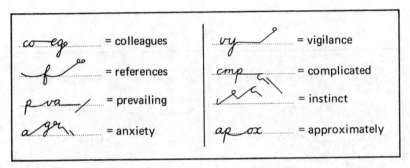

co—ego = colleagues		*vy* = vigilance	
f = references		*cmp* = complicated	
p-va = prevailing		*instinct* = instinct	
a-gr = anxiety		*ap ox* = approximately	

Once more it is a pleasure for myself and my[10] colleagues to present to you at the annual meeting the[20] result which again, I think we may say, is satisfactory.[30] There have been many references in the Press and at[40] our company meetings to the very difficult economic conditions which[50] are prevailing everywhere at the present time. It seems needless[60] for me to say, therefore, that the past year has[70] caused much anxiety. To maintain, but still more to increase,[80] the success of any business is not, even in the[90] most favourable times, an easy task, and that task is[100] not made any lighter in view of the present conditions.[110] It calls for the greatest vigilance in all the vast[120] and complicated details, and it is almost necessary to have[130] an instinct for the movement and development of public taste[140] and demand. I am glad to say the results of[150] the past year's work, which are before you today, give[160] the best indication that we have achieved a measure of[170] success which is in keeping with the effort made.

In[180] the circumstances the business done has been more than satisfactory.[190] It is true that the spending power per head has[200] again diminished slightly and that the number of meals which[210] have been served has also shown a reduction of one[220] per cent. As we served approximately one hundred and fifty[230] million meals, however, we may rest assured that it is[240] not any lack of popularity of our establishments

47

that is[250] the cause of less business. The cause is, without doubt,[260] the general state of trade, and the great amount of[270] unemployment which has been the result.

In contrast to the[280] slight reduction in that side of our business, however, we[290] have served many more people over the counters in our[300] own establishments. The sales of tea, coffee and cocoa have[310] increased considerably and we have also sold more cakes and[320] biscuits. (321)

(Union of Lancashire and Cheshire Institutes)

58

xpe	= expressed	*b*	= Belgian
maj	= major	*p*	= predict
achiev	= achieved	*u*	= uncertain
ov	= overseas	*ap*	= appreciation

Ladies and Gentlemen, A year ago in my Statement I[10] expressed the view that unless we had a major national[20] upset, the coming year should be quite favourable for us.[30] I am, therefore, very happy that this has proved to[40] be the case, and to report that we have achieved[50] an all-time record both in Group turnover and in[60] profits.

The Group net profit, after taxation, is up by[70] one hundred and fifty-five thousand, four hundred and thirty-seven[80] pounds to four hundred and fifty-two thousand, three[90] hundred and twenty-four pounds, and we have been able[100] to transfer the sum of two hundred thousand pounds to[110] the General Reserve Account.

With regard to our overseas companies[120] the year has been somewhat mixed. The results from our[130] South African company were poor, and we have taken steps[140] which will, I hope, ensure a satisfactory profit in future.[150] In my last report I referred to the measures we[160] had taken to improve the position of our Belgian Company,[170] and I am pleased to report that these were most[180] effective and a reasonable profit was made for the year[190] under review.

To predict the results of the year ahead[200] is always difficult, but with the present uncertain economic situation,[210] both at home and abroad, it is almost impossible. Costs[220] in labour and raw materials continue to increase and these[230] will be absorbed as far as possible by improved methods[240] of manufacture and increased sales. I believe the stability of[250] your Company lies in the variety of our products as[260] well as in the great range of industries they serve.[270] So far this year the demand is holding at a[280] satisfactory level, and provided this continues I feel there should[290] be another successful year ahead with further improvement in our[300] trading position.

Once again I wish to record my appreciation[310] to the Staff and Employees for their continued loyal services. (320)

(East Midland Educational Union)

59

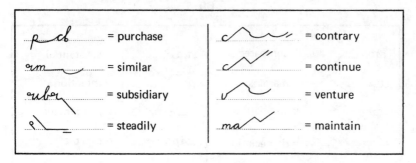

= purchase		= contrary
= similar		= continue
= subsidiary		= venture
= steadily		= maintain

Dear Mr. Smith, I have been interested to read your[10] letter of the 10th of January and to note that[20] your company has under consideration the purchase of another company[30] that produces goods similar to your own. I am glad[40] that you have asked for my advice regarding this matter,[50] because in my opinion it is something about which you[60] must be careful.

I have made a very full examination[70] of the financial position of the company in question, and[80] I am not at all satisfied that the facts and[90] figures which you quote in your letter represent the true[100] position. It is now four years since the undertaking made[110] a real trading profit. The only way in which an[120] open loss was avoided during this period has been through[130] the sale of small subsidiary undertakings. In all cases the[140] subsidiaries which have been sold were themselves making a loss,[150] and were disposed of at a figure well below the[160] value at which they stood in the books of the[170] company.

Your own sales have been increasing steadily for some[180] years, and I do not think that it is necessary[190] for you to buy up the firm in question.

49

On²⁰⁰ the contrary, I am satisfied that if you simply allow²¹⁰ the present position to continue, you will find yourself leading²²⁰ the market, with very little competition from elsewhere.

As you²³⁰ have asked for my opinion, I venture to give it.²⁴⁰ I suggest that instead of buying up a competitor you²⁵⁰ look around and try to find an opportunity to buy²⁶⁰ one of the undertakings that supply you with raw materials.²⁷⁰ In this way you would be able to secure your²⁸⁰ basic requirements at a lower cost and would thus be²⁹⁰ in a position to widen your profit margin. In these³⁰⁰ days most companies find that it becomes more and more³¹⁰ difficult to maintain a reasonable margin of profit. Yours sincerely, (320)

(Pitman Examinations Institute)

60

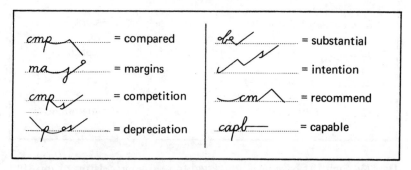

= compared	= substantial
= margins	= intention
= competition	= recommend
= depreciation	= capable

Ladies and Gentlemen, The report and accounts have been in¹⁰ your hands for some time, and as you will have²⁰ seen, there is a fall in the amount of profit³⁰ before taxation of nearly eight hundred thousand pounds when compared⁴⁰ with last year. Those of you who were present at⁵⁰ the meeting last year will remember that I said then⁶⁰ that we must expect a drop in profits, as in⁷⁰ addition to reduced profit margins, arising from keen competition in⁸⁰ the markets we serve, we had to face an increase⁹⁰ in Bank interest and in depreciation.

There has again been¹⁰⁰ a substantial increase in assets, due to the large amount¹¹⁰ of expenditure by the Group on Buildings and Plant. It¹²⁰ is the intention of your Board to undertake a full¹³⁰ review of all the group assets in the current year,¹⁴⁰ and they intend to make such adjustments in the Balance¹⁵⁰ Sheet as they think necessary when the work is finished.¹⁶⁰

Your Directors recommend a final dividend of two and a[170] half per cent, which, with the interim dividend of ten[180] per cent paid on 1st April, makes a total payment[190] of twelve and a half per cent. This compares with[200] a total payment of twenty-two and a half per[210] cent for the previous year.

I have now been with[220] your Company for nearly eight months, and although I have[230] not been able to visit as many Works as I[240] would have liked, I have met most of the senior[250] staff. Although much remains to be done to make many[260] of our activities more efficient and to reduce costs, I[270] am well satisfied that your Company is loyally served by[280] a capable staff and workers.

For the first four months[290] of the current year our sales show an increase of[300] seven per cent over the same period of last year,[310] and your directors are confident that profits will also increase. (320)

(East Midland Educational Union)

61

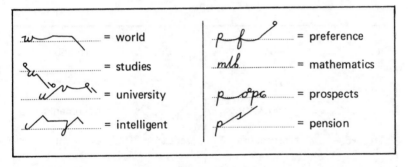

	= world		= preference
	= studies		= mathematics
	= university		= prospects
	= intelligent		= pension

Dear Students, You are now in your last term at[10] school, and I am writing this letter to you so[20] that you will know the kind of opportunity that is[30] waiting for you in the business world. Some of you[40] will, of course, continue your studies and go to a[50] University. This letter is not written for you. It is[60] written for those of you who are leaving school this[70] term and are going out into the world of commerce[80] and industry.

I want to point out to you the[90] advantages that banking can offer as a career. The bank[100] which I represent is looking for young people who are[110] intelligent and who are willing to work hard. Preference will[120] be given to those who have passed their examinations and[130] obtained one or two A level successes. On the other[140] hand, the bank would like also to receive applications from[150] young people who have at least four O level passes[160] to their credit. Students who have obtained good certificates in[170] mathematics and English are particularly welcome.

What does the bank[180] offer you in return for your services? First of all,[190] there is a good training scheme, and you will be[200] paid a full salary during the period of training. The[210] pay is good, and so are the prospects. If you[220] can pass the Bankers' examinations and become a manager you[230] can look forward to a salary of at least two[240] thousand pounds and probably much more. In the meantime our[250] rates of pay compare more than favourably with those in[260] other types of work.

The bank operates an extremely good[270] Pension Scheme, and runs a canteen where cheap but wholesome[280] meals are served throughout the working day. In addition, there[290] are several clubs offering outlets for whatever sport or activity[300] interests you.

Why not fill in the attached form and[310] post it to me at the above address? Yours truly, (320)

(Pitman Examinations Institute)

62

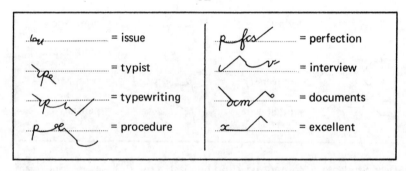

	= issue		= perfection
	= typist		= interview
	= typewriting		= documents
	= procedure		= excellent

Sir, I am writing in reply to your advertisement, which[10] appeared in yesterday's issue of the Daily News, inviting applications[20] for the post of typist and filing clerk. Your advertisement[30] did not state whether you wanted to employ a male[40] or a female, but I am writing in the hope[50] that you prefer to employ a young lady. I set[60] out below some details about myself and my qualifications.

I[70] am seventeen years of age, and three weeks ago I[80] completed a course in typewriting and office procedure. I have[70] two certificates for typewriting, one stating that I achieved a[100] net speed of 52 words a minute for ten[110] minutes and the other stating I achieved $99^{120} \cdot 5$ per cent accuracy on the perfection test, which[130] lasted for a quarter of an hour. I also have[140] a first-class pass in Office Practice, the subjects covered[150] by the examination being filing, making telephone calls, and sending[160] cables and telegrams, and other points such as how to[170] behave when dealing with people, and so on.

I have[180] no references from previous employers because, if you offer me[190] employment, it will be my first post. I hope[200] you will consider this application favourably, and will grant me an[210] interview because I very much enjoy typewriting and would be[220] most happy to be employed in an office to produce[230] typewritten documents of one kind and another.

I think it[240] may be of interest if I add that I have[250] an excellent knowledge of the French language. This is because[260] my mother is French, and throughout my life I have[270] heard French spoken in the home. I am therefore able[280] to speak and write French as easily as I can[290] speak and write English.

If you grant me an interview[300] I shall come into the city by bus, arriving either[310] at 10 a.m. or 3 p.m. Yours faithfully, (320)

(Pitman Examinations Institute)

63

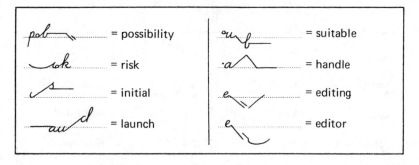

= possibility	= suitable
= risk	= handle
= initial	= editing
= launch	= editor

Dear Brown, I have for some time past been giving[10] very careful thought to the possibility of this Publishing House[20] entering the field of periodicals. I realize only too well[30] that this is an entirely new venture, and it is[40] not possible to rule out entirely the risk of failure.[50] I have, however, managed to convince my fellow-directors on[60] the Board that the idea is worth a trial because,[70] if we succeed in interesting the reading public, large profits[80] can be made. We have therefore decided to risk a[90] small expenditure in the hope of making a large profit.[100]

You will understand that we do not wish our initial[110] expenses to be greater than is absolutely necessary. This is[120] where you, as our Personnel Manager, can probably assist us.[130] The first periodical we have planned to launch will be[140] a monthly called "Science and Your Life". The idea is[150] to have a sixteen-page magazine at the beginning, increasing[160] the size if it becomes popular. The contents would be[170] varied but would mainly cover new discoveries in industry, science,[180] or medicine that are likely to be of interest to[190] the general public.

What I want you to do is[200] to find out whether we already have on our staff[210] suitable people to handle such a periodical. I think you[220] could possibly approach this question in two ways. First, are[230] there in any of our departments three or four young[240] men who would be willing to contribute lively articles covering[250] current discoveries? Secondly, have we on our staff any people[260] whose duties do not fully occupy their time and who[270] could reasonably be asked to do extra work in connection[280] with editing and production, etc?

If we could find on[290] our own staff in this way a band of workers,[300] it would then be necessary to engage only an Editor[310] from outside.

Will you report to me, please? Yours sincerely, (320)

(Pitman Examinations Institute)

64

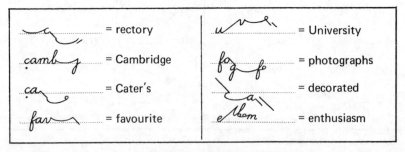

= rectory		= University	
= Cambridge		= photographs	
= Cater's		= decorated	
= favourite		= enthusiasm	

They had been happy years, those of Dick's education with[10] Jim at the Rectory. Today, in his last year, he[20] looked back on them as he walked home down the[30] lane, for they had come to an end.

In the[40] autumn he and Jim were to go up to Cambridge.[50] This was due to Mrs. Cater's generosity. Dick was a[60] favourite of hers, and he had shown such promise that[70] she had begged his father to let her pay the[80] fees and send him to the University.

He looked back[90] on happy years between the Rectory and the farm; the[100] Rector's study with its friendly fire, or in the summer[110] the jar full of gay flowers, the family photographs, and[120] the walls lined with books. There was something noble about[130] that room, with its air of quiet thought, so different[140] from the parlour at Folly Farm, simple, just a resting[150] place after labour.

To Dick, looking back over the last[160] few years, the time spent in that room seemed but[170] an hour, and in that hour the rows of books[180] on the shelves, at which he had taken a quick[190] look on that first October morning, had grown from mere[200] words and names into old friends. The room was no[210] longer a place of walls, but of voices from the[220] depths of time.

At any passage in a book with[230] which he was particularly pleased, the Rector used to seize[240] a pencil from his pocket and score it heavily. It[250] was a life habit, so by now nearly every page[260] was decorated with double upright strokes in the margins and[270] notes written by him in any blank space. He argued[280] with long-dead authors all up and down their pages.[290]

Dick's most happy memories were of the hours spent over[300] Shakespeare's plays, which they read, dividing the characters among the[310] three of them, until the Rector's enthusiasm infected them all. (320)

(East Midland Educational Union)

65

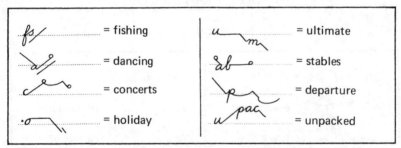

= fishing	= ultimate
= dancing	= stables
= concerts	= departure
= holiday	= unpacked

When the question of summer holidays arose it was very[10] difficult for the family to decide where to go. Jack[20] wanted to go to a place where he could take[30] long walks or go fishing or horse-riding. Jane said[40] she would like a lively place where she could practise[50] her dancing and attend concerts and lectures. Mother and Father[60] wanted a quiet holiday where they could relax in the[70] sun and forget the many worries that occurred at home.[80]

The family did not really want to separate, however, so[90] there was much discussion about the various places which were[100] suggested. At last a decision was reached, and a town[110] by the sea was the ultimate choice. Here there would[120] be pleasant sandy beaches where Mother and Father could rest[130] in deck-chairs, or they could wander in the attractive[140] park and admire the well-stocked flower beds.

At the[150] same time there was a large pavilion and concert hall[160] where Jane would be able to dance and listen to[170] her favourite music being played by good orchestras and sung[180] by well-known singers. For Jack there was beautiful country[190] quite near to the town, also riding stables where horses[200] could be hired, and nearby historical places that were within[210] walking distance.

Having settled the place the question then arose[220] as to when the family should take their holiday. June[230] was suggested as the month when the weather should be[240] at its best and the seaside resort not too crowded.[250]

As the departure date drew near activity at home increased[260] and each member of the family was busy making preparations[270] for the journey which was to be made by car.[280] This proved very enjoyable as the day was fine, sunny[290] and warm.

On arrival at their hotel they quickly unpacked[300] and went out to walk along the shore. They were[310] certain they were going to have a very pleasant holiday. (320)

(Pitman Examinations Institute)

66

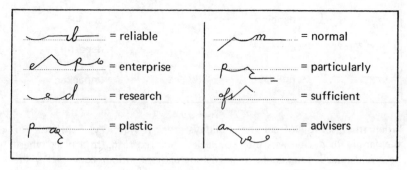

Dear Mr. Brown, I understand from a reliable source that[10] you are willing to invest a considerable sum of money[20] in a new enterprise, if there is reasonable security for[30] your money and the risk is not too great. I[40] may mention that several other names have been given to[50] me, but I am writing to you first because the[60] amount of money that has been suggested is more or[70] less in line with what would be required for the[80] project I have in mind.

I am at present head[90] of the Research Department of one of the leading chemists[100] of this country, and I have recently invented a new[110] plastic material. This material is just as flexible as those[120] already on the market and is completely unbreakable, but in[130] addition it has the advantage that it can be moulded[140] into a much greater variety of shapes and will keep[150] the desired shape under all normal conditions. This plastic can[160] be made up in a wonderful range of colours, and[170] furthermore, patterns of different colours can be built into the[180] material.

My company is not particularly interested in the development[190] of this material as they quite reasonably claim that their[200] present plastics are selling widely and are earning large profits[210] for the organization. They are not willing at present to[220] invest in new machinery, etc. In the circumstances I would[230] like to start my own company. I have sufficient capital[240] to start in a small way, but I strongly believe[250] that this new company should be launched on a large[260] scale. Ample supplies should be manufactured and distributed throughout the[270] country, and then there should be a nation-wide advertising[280] campaign, using the press and television.

May I suggest that[290] you arrange to visit me, bringing with you some trusted[300] advisers? I would then display my work to you, and[310] unfold my full plans for your careful consideration. Yours faithfully, (320)

(Pitman Examinations Institute)

67

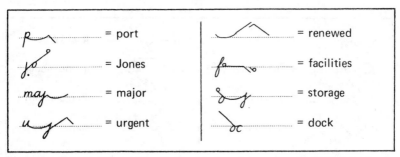

= port		= renewed	
= Jones		= facilities	
= major		= storage	
= urgent		= dock	

I now wish to refer to the report of the[10] special committee. This committee was set up last year to[20] look into the possibilities of further development of our Port.[30] The chairman of the Port Development Committee is Mr. James[40] Brown, and there are six other members, two of them[50] being experts in the field of public transport. The company[60] which at present runs the Port is also represented on[70] the Committee. Mrs. Mary Jones and Major Peter Smith are[80] the members of the Committee appointed to represent the interests[90] of users of the Port.

I am certain all will[100] agree that we should thank the Committee for having produced[110] this report in such a short time. Of course, it[120] is an urgent matter because we must reach a decision[130] on the running of the Port before the company's contract[140] comes to an end in six months' time. I am[150] very pleased that the report of the Committee is to[160] the effect that the Port Management Company should have its[170] contract renewed. I am also pleased to note that only[180] minor changes in the terms of the contract are proposed.[190] I have been told by the Chairman of the Port[200] Management Company that he and the other members of the[210] Board of Directors will accept these changes. This is very[220] good news for it means that we can look forward[230] to another period of development of our Port facilities.

The[240] last ten years have seen great changes. For example, there[250] has been a twenty-five per cent increase in the[260] berthing space available for ships, and there has been a[270] forty per cent increase in storage space so that very[280] large quantities of goods waiting to be loaded on to[290] the ships can be kept under cover.

The Chairman of[300] the Port Management Company has said that a further increase[310] in Port capacity is planned. A large dock is to[320] be built soon for the use of very big ships. (330)

(Pitman Examinations Institute)

68

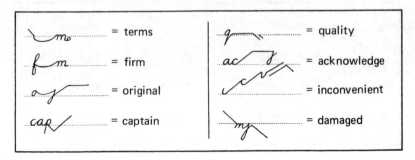

= terms		= quality	
= firm		= acknowledge	
= original		= inconvenient	
= captain		= damaged	

58

When goods are to be sent from one place to[10] another by sea, the most important of the papers that[20] must be drawn up is the Bill of Lading. This[30] acts as a receipt for the goods which are to[40] be carried. It also states the terms under which the[50] goods are to be carried, and, in addition to these[60] two things, it can be used to show who is[70] the owner of the goods themselves.

These Bills, as a[80] general rule, are made out in sets of three. One[90] is sent by post to the firm or person who[100] is to receive the goods, one is sent by the[110] same ship, and the other is kept for reference. These[120] three are all original papers. Some copies also are made[130] and one of these is kept by the agent of[140] the ship and is given to the Captain with the[150] other ship's papers. If the shipping of the goods has[160] been arranged by brokers, a further copy will be kept[170] by them.

There are various types of Bills of Lading:[180] some have a note on them to the effect that[190] the value and quality and even the nature of the[200] contents is not known. Some acknowledge the fact that the[210] goods have been put on board the ship; this seems[220] to be satisfactory, but delays due to various matters may[230] mean that the Bill of Lading may not be available[240] to be sent until after the arrival of the goods[250] themselves. This, of course, may be very inconvenient and may[260] even cause a delay in the delivery of the cargo.[270] To meet this difficulty another Bill to say that the[280] goods have been received for shipment is sometimes used, but[290] this is not recommended by the banks as it does[300] not show that the goods have been shipped: in fact[310] they could have been lost or damaged before they were[320] loaded. When the goods are known to have been put[330] on the ship in a damaged state, the master of[340] the ship may say so on the Bill of Lading. (350)

(London Chamber of Commerce)

69

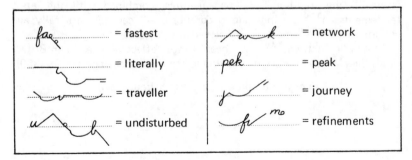

= fastest	= network
= literally	= peak
= traveller	= journey
= undisturbed	= refinements

Business travel has grown rapidly in recent years on a[10] scale which has made it one of the fastest-developing[20] sections of the British travel industry.

Time is literally money[30] to the business traveller and he demands a high standard[40] of efficiency from a transport organization. A very reliable and[50] high-speed service, based on a timetable suited to his[60] special requirements, is essential. The busy and well-paid traveller[70] represents a multi-million-pound market, and all forms of[80] transport compete for his patronage.

The business traveller generally has[90] to work during his journey and therefore requires a high[100] standard of accommodation combined with a calm and undisturbed atmosphere.[110] Catering facilities of a similar standard are also important.

British[120] Rail are determined to provide services and facilities which meet[130] these exacting requirements, and are endeavouring to expand their share[140] of the business travel market, confident of their ability to[150] provide a service which, in terms of convenience, is superior[160] to other forms of transport.

The Inter-City network of[170] British Rail covers more than one hundred stations in the[180] main centres of industry and population. Within this network, high[190]-speed trains operate an all-the-year-round service specially[200] designed to meet the requirements of businessmen, and many trains[210] on Inter-City services achieve and maintain speeds of a[220] hundred miles per hour.

Inter-City travel reaches its peak[230] in speed and comfort on the routes served by Pullman[240] trains. These are the fastest trains on the routes, and[250] complete a journey of nearly two hundred miles in only[260] two-and-a-half hours.

These Pullman trains were specially[270] designed for high-speed running, and great care was taken[280] to provide a quiet and comfortable ride for the passengers.[290] The interior of the carriages has been planned to retain[300] the traditional Pullman features, combined with the latest refinements in[310] fittings and decorations. All carriages are fully air-conditioned and[320] meals can be served at every seat.

The Pullman trains[330] have been a most effective weapon in British Rail's fight[340] to improve its position in the field of business travel. (350)

(Yorkshire Council for Further Education)

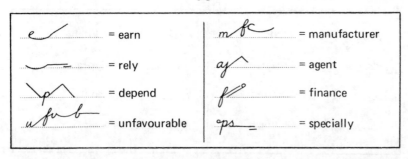

e⟋ = earn	⟋ = manufacturer
= rely	= agent
= depend	= finance
= unfavourable	= specially

Many people earn their living by taking part in the[10] business of bringing goods into the country and selling and[20] shipping goods to people who are in other countries. This[30] is a very important kind of trade. Countries rely on[40] each other to supply the things that they need, such[50] as food and raw materials. But they cannot buy the[60] things they want from each other without selling things also.[70] They depend upon each other for markets and this is[80] known as the Balance of Trade. This balance is brought[90] about by setting against each other all the goods sold[100] out of the country, and all the goods brought into[110] it. If the balance is favourable it means that they[120] have sold more than they have bought. If it is[130] unfavourable, they have bought more than they have sold. There[140] is also a Balance of Payments. This, in fact, is[150] the. Balance of Trade with all the services that are[160] sold and bought added to it; such services as shipping[170] and insurance are often bought and sold between countries. The[180] Balance of Payments shows what we really owe to other[190] countries, or what they owe to us. The Balance of[200] Trade shows only whether more goods have been bought or[210] sold.

The manufacturer who is making goods for the export[220] market may sell his goods to someone else who will[230] then do all the work of storing and packing, shipping[240] and selling. But many manufacturers get an agent to do[250] these jobs for them and they themselves continue to own[260] the goods until they are sold to a customer in[270] another country. These agents have several different names and do[280] different work, and more than one agent may be concerned[290] in any given deal. Usually there are agents and merchants[300] in the country from which the goods are being sold[310] and in the country where they are being bought, and[320] they keep the manufacturer in touch with the buyer. For[330] payment, business men make great use of the banks and[340] finance houses that deal specially in this kind of work. (350)

(London Chamber of Commerce)

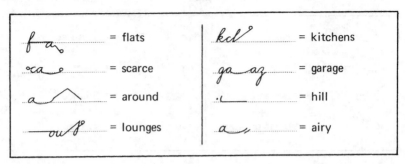

	= flats		= kitchens
	= scarce		= garage
	= around		= hill
	= lounges		= airy

It is interesting to see from today's issue of the[10] local paper that several new properties have been put on[20] to the market. Unfortunately, most of the houses and flats[30] that are now being offered are rather expensive. This is[40] not surprising, however, when we remember how scarce property has[50] become in and around this city.

Six blocks of flats[60] are now being offered, all within five miles of the[70] centre of the city. Of these there are two blocks[80] which seem to offer good value for money. The first[90] is a block of twenty units on the south side[100] of the city. The number of bedrooms per flat varies[110] from two to four but in all other respects the[120] flats have the same accommodation.

The lounges are very large[130] and have small verandahs looking out over the neighbouring hills.[140] The kitchens are extremely modern and convenient, and they contain[150] several fittings not normally found in flats of this size.[160]

The twenty flats are for sale on leases of ninety[170]-nine years and cost from seven thousand five hundred pounds[180] for a two-bedroomed flat to nine thousand five hundred[190] pounds for four bedrooms. Garage space is provided at basement[200] level.

The second block of flats to which reference has[210] been made stands on a hill in the eastern area.[220] Advantage has been taken of the slope of the land[230] to set out the property in a most attractive manner.[240] This scheme is a large one, and provision has been[250] made for one hundred and twenty units, of which eighty[260] are now ready for occupation. The flats are in blocks[270] of five, with one flat to each floor. This allows[280] for a maximum of window space, making the rooms light[290] and airy. The flats on the ground floor and the[300] first floor contain two bedrooms while those on the upper[310] floors each contain three. Garages have been built at the[320] rear. Plenty of open space surrounds the property, and the[330] flats are excellent value at from five thousand pounds to[340] six thousand pounds, according to size and position. It is[350] understood that thirty of the flats have already been sold. (360)

(Pitman Examinations Institute)

72

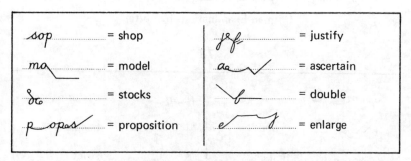

ᴀᴏᴘ = shop		= justify	
ᴍᴀ = model		= ascertain	
ᴅᴄ = stocks		= double	
ᴘᴏᴘᴀᴅ = proposition		= enlarge	

Dear Sirs, You are, of course, aware that I have[10] for some years sold your products in my shop in[20] this busy High Street. I have always kept a large[30] stock of your various goods, and I have made a[40] point never to continue to sell any article if your[50] firm has brought out a new or improved model. As[60] your range of products increases I have, however, found that[70] it is extremely expensive to carry such large stocks. If,[80] on the other hand, I reduced important stocks, it would[90] mean keeping a customer waiting for a week or two[100] while I waited for delivery of the item from you.[110]

I have given this matter much thought, and I now[120] wish to make a proposition. This is that I should[130] cease to be a general trader, selling goods from other[140] manufacturers than yourselves. Instead, this shop should become a branch[150] of your London stores, financed by you and managed by[160] me. I should, of course, require a commission on all[170] sales, in addition to my salary as manager. I am[180] confident that the volume of my sales would justify your[190] taking this step.

You can, of course, consult your own[200] books in order to ascertain my purchases from you over[210] the last five years. To assist you, however, I am[220] enclosing figures which will show you not only my purchases[230] from you but also my monthly sales. You will see[240] that these sales have been steadily increasing. This increase has[250] been so large recently that the sales figures for last[260] year are more than double those for five years ago.[270]

63

I am also enclosing for your information details of the[280] overhead costs of running these premises. The lease of the[290] shop still has ten years to run, and the rent[300] is very reasonable because the agreement was entered into fifteen[310] years ago, when prices were not as high as they[320] are today. It would in my opinion be desirable to[330] enlarge the store rooms at the back of the shop,[340] however, as these tend to become crowded with stock.

I[350] shall be very interested to hear your views. Yours faithfully, (360)

(Pitman Examinations Institute)

73

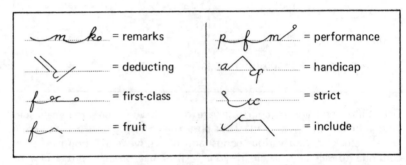

= remarks	= performance
= deducting	= handicap
= first-class	= strict
= fruit	= include

In the course of his remarks the Chairman said: Ladies[10] and Gentlemen, Last year I mentioned that the Company's net[20] contribution to the balance of payments amounted to a very[30] large sum. This had been arrived at by way of[40] deducting total expenditure on imported raw materials and overseas investments[50] from the total income. Our income came from dividends, exports[60] of manufactured goods, machinery and supplies, and certain other sources.[70] Although our factories have played their part by producing first-[80] class goods for export, the major portion of these earnings[90] naturally results from the activities of the subsidiary and associated[100] companies. Of course, this income is the fruit of investment[110] in the past — sometimes in the very distant past. The[120] return on these invested savings has been, as far as[130] we are concerned, very satisfactory both to the Company and[140] to the country as a whole. But despite our fine[150] performance in the past, often in the face of strong[160] competition, and even taking into account the present very healthy[170] prospects of your Company, foreign investment remains very much out[180] of favour with the Government at the moment. Another handicap[190] we suffer in common with other companies is restraint in[200] developing or adding to our overseas businesses. The acquisition of[210] new businesses by your Company, whether in the particular field[220] in which we deal or, for that matter, in any[230] other industry, is subject nowadays to very strict controls.

Turning[240] now to the Balance Sheet, you will have noticed that[250] last year we had invested slightly less than fifty million[260] pounds. While this is a significant figure in itself, it[270] is still not large in relation to the Group as[280] a whole. By far the greater part of this investment[290] comes under the heading of Trade Investments. The sales figures[300] of these companies are, therefore, not included in the figures[310] of Group turnover which include only the turnover of subsidiaries.[320] To achieve our objective on a large scale must take[330] quite a number of years as time is needed both[340] to develop existing interests and to make the right kinds[350] of acquisitions. Your Directors are very confident of the future. (360)

(Pitman Examinations Institute)

74

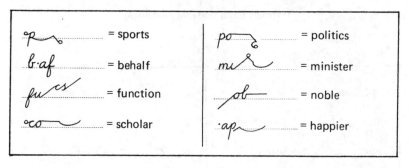

= sports		= politics
= behalf		= minister
= function		= noble
= scholar		= happier

I am happy to be present today at the Annual[10] General Meeting of the School Sports Club. You were kind[20] enough a year ago to elect me as your Chairman,[30] and I have followed the activities of the Club, with[40] much interest. It was a great disappointment to me that[50] I was not able to attend the Annual Competitions held[60] in June. As you know, I am a business man,[70] and I was at that time travelling abroad on behalf[80] of my company. You have, however, paid me the honour[90] of asking me to continue as your Chairman for another[100] year, and I certainly hope that it will be possible[110] for me to attend more of your functions in the[120] coming months.

65

You have, of course, only to look at[130] me to realize that it is many years since I[140] was a scholar at this school. In fact, 34[150] years have passed since I left at the age of[160] sixteen to attend another College, and and from there I went[170] on to University. You see, therefore, if you can do[180] a simple addition sum, that I am now 50 years[190] of age.

It is of interest to wonder what the[200] boys sitting in front of me will have become by[210] the time they reach the age of 50. Some of[220] you will no doubt be business men like me. Others[230] of you will perhaps enter politics. There may even be[240] a future Prime Minister sitting before me at this moment.[250] Some of you will be scientists, and some will be[260] engineers. I hope most sincerely, however, that among you there[270] are some who will become teachers. Teaching is a noble[280] profession, and it is a sad thing when a country[290] finds itself in the position of having too few teachers.[300] We have to admit that not everyone benefits from education,[310] but the great mass of the people lead much fuller[320] and happier lives because they have had the advantages of[330] a good general education. Part of a general education is[340] to learn to be a good sportsman, and members of[350] this School Sports Club are, indeed, learning to be that. (360)

(Pitman Examinations Institute)

75

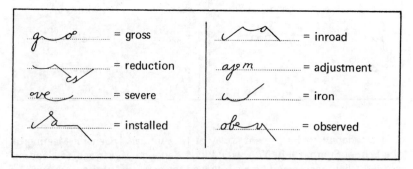

= gross	= inroad
= reduction	= adjustment
= severe	= iron
= installed	= observed

I am sure that you will all be interested to[10] know that the gross trading profit of the company for[20] the year was eight hundred thousand pounds. This figure must[30] be compared with a gross profit of just over one[40] million pounds for the previous year. The net result will[50] not, however, be very different from that of last year[60] as smaller sums are being set aside for depreciation and[70] for tax.

You will want to be given some reason[80] for the reduction in the gross trading profit, however. First[90] of all, the reduction is partly the result of the[100] increased competition with which we have been faced. This competition[110] has been particularly severe in the export markets of the[120] company. We had an excellent turnover but prices were unfortunately[130] rather low.

Another reason for the fall in gross profit[140] was the rise in the prices of most of our[150] raw materials. Rates of pay were also increased, and we[160] found that the costs of operating our new plant were[170] much higher than was expected when the plant was first[180] installed. In addition, there was a break-down of one[190] of our more important older machines. All these items taken[200] together made a heavy inroad into our profits. The prophecy[210] of a year ago, therefore, that you could look forward[220] to better results in the year under review has not[230] been justified.

Your directors are, however, recommending the same dividend[240] as was paid to you last year, namely seven per[250] cent for the year. They are able to do this[260] because, as I said just now, various adjustments have been[270] made in the amounts set aside for depreciation, tax, bad[280] debts, etc., and the net profit justifies the payment of[290] this dividend.

The selling prices of the company's products in[300] the home markets are fixed by the iron and steel[310] board. A general increase in prices was granted as from[320] the first of April last. Some companies, however, have not[330] observed this price increase, and we have consequently been faced[340] with competition from companies charging lower prices than those which[350] were agreed with the board. This is an unfortunate matter. (360)

(Pitman Examinations Institute)

76

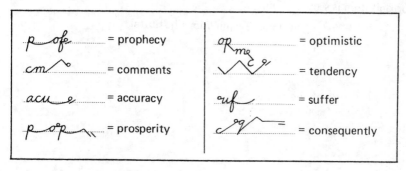

= prophecy	= optimistic
= comments	= tendency
= accuracy	= suffer
= prosperity	= consequently

I know that it is usual to include a prophecy[10] about the future in an address of this kind. No[20] doubt, therefore, you are expecting me to make some comments[30] on our prospects during the current financial year. It is[40] perhaps easy to foresee the future in the case of[50] some types of industry, where conditions do not vary much[60] from season to season. In an industry such as ours,[70] however, it is impossible to forecast with any degree of[80] accuracy what is likely to happen many months ahead.

We[90] are very dependent upon the conditions prevailing in the country[100] as a whole because the demand for motor cars varies[110] with the prosperity of the people. We in our turn[120] are dependent upon the prosperity of the motor industry, as[130] they are the principal buyers of our safety glass. We[140] have just had a very good year, and I do[150] not wish to appear unduly optimistic when I say that[160] I think that the demand for our products will increase[170] still further in the current year.

We are now feeling[180] the full benefit of the reduction in prices which was[190] made last July. As a result of that reduction demand[200] increased and our total profits rose. In my opinion that[210] tendency will continue. As we still have some unused capacity[220] in our factories we shall be able to meet larger[230] purchases without becoming involved in heavy capital expenditure.

I must[240] add one word of warning, however. We are affected in[250] many ways by the general economic conditions. Our future can[260] be seriously influenced by changes in interest rates and by[270] changes in the rate of Purchase Tax on articles using[280] safety glass. If interest rates rise or if there is[290] an increase in Purchase Tax we shall suffer. On the[300] other hand, I am bound to say that there are[310] no immediate signs of any such changes taking place. There[320] has recently been a great improvement in the country's financial[330] position, and the value of sterling has been well-maintained[340] throughout the year. You may, therefore, leave this hall feeling[350] fairly confident that the future of this organization is secure. (360)

(Pitman Examinations Institute)

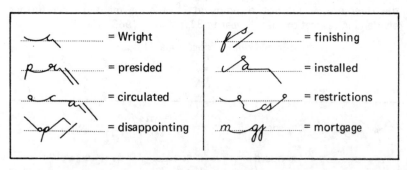

= Wright		= finishing	
= presided		= installed	
= circulated		= restrictions	
= disappointing		= mortgage	

The 28th annual general meeting of Wright & Sons[10] Limited was held yesterday in London, when the Chairman and[20] Managing Director presided. The following is an extract from his[30] circulated statement.

As I stated in my interim report in[40] March, the profits are less than those for the previous[50] year, when record figures were reported, but, at the same[60] time, although disappointing, they may be considered to be fairly[70] good when compared with those of the year before.

The[80] sales of the Kitchen Division, which is now based at[90] the Walton factory, have been maintained, and the new finishing[100] process which we installed is now producing results, but the[110] cost of manufacture is continuing to rise steeply, and by[120] the nature of our business in a very keen market,[130] most of these increases have had to be absorbed.

The[140] total sales of the Group for the year were slightly[150] less than those for the previous year, although the Kitchen[160] Division showed an increase, even when the restrictions imposed on[170] the building industry had begun to take effect. In the[180] first three months of the current year the total sales[190] were almost the same as for the corresponding three months[200] last year.

It is difficult to predict the future trend,[210] as costs continue to rise and profit margins are under[220] heavy pressure. In the Kitchen Division, depending as we do[230] on the building industry, the lack of confidence in the[240] Government now shown by the builders, and the difficulty which[250] the prospective house buyer has in trying to raise a[260] mortgage, suggest that business is not going to be easy.[270]

In order to take advantage of the taxation terms of[280] the Finance Act of 1965, an[290] Interim Dividend of 22½ per cent[300] subject to income tax, and which was the same as[310] the total dividend for last year, was paid on the[320] 4th of April, 1966. At that[330] time it was stated that the directors would not recommend[340] the payment of any further dividend in respect of the[350] year to 31st March, 1966. (360)

(East Midland Educational Union)

78

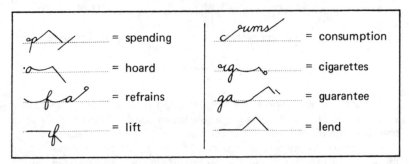

= spending		= consumption
= hoard		= cigarettes
= refrains		= guarantee
= lift		= lend

When a man says that he is saving a certain[10] part of his income he means that he is not[20] spending it. This does not mean that no use is[30] being made of it. He does not usually bury his[40] savings in the garden, or hoard them in a money[50] box. Instead he lends the money to a bank, or[60] a building society, or to the Government, or to people[70] who need capital to finance their business. The man who[80] saves refrains from buying the new clothes or car that[90] he might have bought, and instead the business that borrows[100] his money uses it to buy tools or machinery, or[110] to install a lift or build a new workshop. There[120] are thus two kinds of demand. One is for consumption[130] goods, that is for the things people buy to satisfy[140] their personal wants. The other is for capital goods, that[150] is for all the various stores and equipment that are[160] wanted in production. What a person, therefore, thinks of as[170] saving is, from the point of view of society as[180] a whole, simply another form of spending.

When we buy[190] goods for our own use we do so because we[200] believe that they will satisfy our wants; but when a[210] business man buys tools or equipment he does so in[220] order to produce more cheaply, or more efficiently, or in[230] greater quantities, the goods that later he hopes to sell[240] at a profit. He does not want the tools for[250] their own sake as we want the food or cigarettes[260] we buy, but only for the part they will play[270] in making other things. This means that his willingness to[280] buy machinery depends on his prospects of selling his products,[290] and if he is uncertain whether or not he will[300] be able to do so, he may buy only

70

a[310] small amount of equipment this year, until he has a[320] chance to see how trade goes. There is, therefore, at[330] any one time no guarantee that all the money people[340] save from their incomes and are prepared to lend is,[350] in fact, invested in the purchase of more capital goods. (360)

(Pitman Examinations Institute)

79

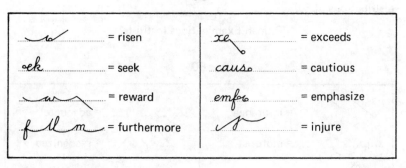

(shorthand)	= risen	*(shorthand)*	= exceeds
(shorthand)	= seek	*(shorthand)*	= cautious
(shorthand)	= reward	*(shorthand)*	= emphasize
(shorthand)	= furthermore	*(shorthand)*	= injure

The Chairman pointed out that the company had had a[10] very satisfactory year on the whole. During the year there[20] had been a considerable increase in the gross income of[30] the company. The income had, in fact, risen by more[40] than 25 per cent. The reason for this increase[50] was not far to seek. The company took great care[60] to choose its investments very wisely, and it was reaping[70] the reward for this cautious policy. The higher income was[80] brought about by increases in nearly all the dividends received.[90] Furthermore, there was a good return on the new investments[100] made last September, and the total number of dividends received[110] during the year greatly exceeds that for the previous year.[120]

The Chairman continued by saying: We have already been able[130] to pay the same half-yearly dividend as last year,[140] and in addition your Board has now recommended the same[150] final dividend. The total for the year, therefore, is 12[160]½ per cent, which is made up of[170] an interim dividend of 6½ per cent[180] and the final payment of 6 per cent. There is[190] no doubt that you will regard this result with general[200] satisfaction in view of the present restrictions.

However, it would[210] not be fair of me this afternoon if I neglected[220] to emphasize the effect that the recent Budget is likely[230] to have upon our undertaking. This is particularly so in[240] the matter of overseas investments. It is strange that the[250] Government has seen fit to injure the prospects of the[260] company in this way, in view of the fact that[270] we bring into this country large amounts of foreign currency.[280] We shall have to bear in mind the new provisions[290] of the Budget when we seek out new investments. It[300] is inevitable that more of our capital will in future[310] have to be invested in the home country, and there[320] is every possibility that the return in the form of[330] dividends will be lower.

It will be of some interest[340] to shareholders to add that our ratio of profit to[350] expenses is excellent, enabling us to make very good distributions. (360)

(Pitman Examinations Institute)

80

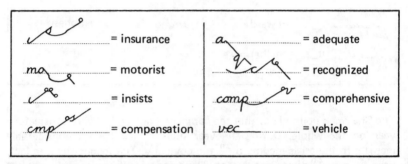

= insurance		= adequate	
= motorist		= recognized	
= insists		= comprehensive	
= compensation		= vehicle	

There are two types of Insurance for the private motorist.[10] One is known as "Third Party" and the other as[20] "Full Comprehensive." All that the law insists upon is that[30] you take out a policy giving third-party cover. This[40] means that if you kill or injure someone, you have[50] insurance to ensure that compensation can be paid. The person[60] involved may be a pedestrian, the owner of another vehicle,[70] a passenger in your own car, or any other person.[80] Third-party insurance is strictly limited to claims by a[90] third-party, and does not cover the cost of any[100] damage sustained by you, your car, or your property. All[110] motor vehicles licensed for use on public roads must be[120] covered by insurance for third-party, and unless adequate insurance[130] has been arranged with a recognized company a Road Fund[140] Licence will not be issued.

The second type of Insurance,[150] Full Comprehensive, is the better of the two, because it[160] not only gives cover against third-party claims likely to[170] arise as the result of an accident but it also[180] includes provision for compensation for any damage caused to your[190] own car or to yourself.

In order that an owner[200] may not be inconvenienced when taking out a new policy,[210] an insurance company or Broker will issue a temporary certificate[220] of insurance. The normal cover note expires after thirty days,[230] but is acceptable to the authorities, and so permits the[240] use of a vehicle on the road whilst a new[250] policy and official certificate are in the course of preparation.[260]

Premiums quoted are normally for a period of one year,[270] but shorter periods can be arranged at special rates. A[280] company's quotation can be reduced in many ways, such as[290] an agreement by you to pay the first few pounds[300] of any claim. A discount can also be arranged if[310] you limit the use of your vehicle to one named[320] driver. A third way is to drive so carefully that[330] after completing one year without an accident involving any claim,[340] you would, thereby, qualify for a discount on renewal of[350] your insurance. This is known as a "No Claims Bonus." (360)

(Welsh Joint Education Committee)

81

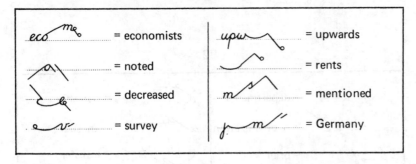

= economists	= upwards
= noted	= rents
= decreased	= mentioned
= survey	= Germany

The value of money, we are told, is indicated by[10] what a given amount of money will buy. Economists are[20] interested in finding out how the value of money changes[30] as the years go by. They do this by taking[40] a group of items and noting the prices paid for[50] such goods and services at a certain date. Then, at[60] a later date, current prices for the same group of[70] items are noted and compared with those of the original[80] period. In this way it can be seen whether a[90] given amount of money can buy as much now as[100] it did, say, five years ago. If, for example, a[110] pound note obtains for the buyer less now than it[120] would have done last year, we can say that the[130] cost of living has gone up or the value of[140] the pound has decreased.

A recent survey of the way[150] prices have increased all over the world has shown that[160] the cost of living in most countries is still rising.[170] In some countries the increase in the cost of living[180] has been very great. In one South American country, the[190] cost of living figure last year was 100; today[200] it has reached the figure of 219.[210] In the United Kingdom, the cost of living has been[220] moving upwards at a steady rate since the last war.[230] Compared with two years ago, the cost of living has[240] increased by about four per cent. That is to say,[250] the average family is spending an extra 50p each[260] week because of the higher prices of foodstuffs, and because[270] of the increased rents and rates.

At the same time,[280] wages have been increased for large numbers of people. Earlier,[290] we mentioned the case of the South American country where[300] the cost of living had risen very steeply. In the[310] same country, the wage level of industrial workers has increased[320] from 100 three years ago to 246[330] now. In West Germany, too, wages have risen[340] by about five per cent, yet the cost of living[350] is only two per cent higher for the same period. (360)

(Pitman Examinations Institute)

82

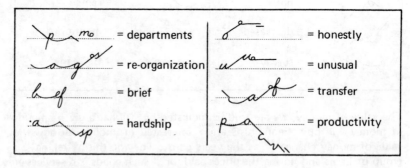

= departments	= honestly
= re-organization	= unusual
= brief	= transfer
= hardship	= productivity

The enclosed statement is sent to you and to all[10] heads of departments at the request of the managing director.[20] As you are all well aware, this company has been[30] going through a difficult time during the last two or[40] three years. After careful consideration, the Board of Directors has[50] decided that a complete re-organization is necessary.

Each head of[60] a department is, therefore, being asked to submit a report[70] on the working of his section. In the first place,[80] a list should be compiled of all the members of[90] his staff, together with a brief account of their duties.[100] Then, suggestions should be made for the reduction of staff.[110] The members of the Board are careful to point out[120] that they do not wish to cause hardship, but in[130] times of prosperity it is easy for a situation to[140] develop in which a department is greatly over-staffed. An[150] opportunity must now be taken to look more closely into[160] this matter and to see whether it is possible for[170] some of the younger members of the staff to be[180] released and their work shared among the older ones. This[190] report on the work of the staff should be compiled honestly,[200] and personal feelings should not be allowed to enter into[210] it. It must be remembered that it is not intended[220] to dismiss staff except in the most unusual circumstances. In[230] the majority of cases it will be found possible to[240] transfer men who are not needed in one department into[250] another section where their services are required.

Secondly, all heads[260] of departments are requested to give thorough consideration to their[270] routine methods of work and try to find ways of[280] working in a more economical fashion. The overheads of the[290] company have been very high for some years, and recently[300] they have increased out of all proportion to any increase[310] in productivity. This state of affairs cannot be allowed to[320] continue. The Board of Directors do not wish to engage[330] the services of outside experts to suggest ways and means[340] of saving time and money. They prefer to have the[350] advice of all those who are actually doing the work. (360)

(Pitman Examinations Institute)

83

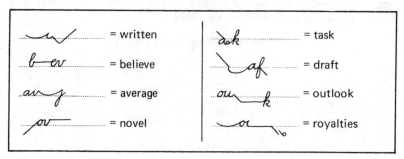

⌇	= written	⌇	= task
⌇	= believe	⌇	= draft
⌇	= average	⌇	= outlook
⌇	= novel	⌇	= royalties

People who have never written a book and never could[10] write a book often believe that authors make a great[20] deal of money from their writing. In a few cases[30] this is quite true. A writer who is very success-ful[40] can make a lot of money, particularly if his books[50] are translated into many different languages and are sold throughout[60] the world. If one of the big film companies buys[70] the rights of his book in order to make a[80] film of it, he can indeed be considered a fortunate[90] person.

Success such as this, however, comes to only a[100] very few out of the thousands who have their work[110] published in the course of a year. It has been[120] estimated that the average person who produces a novel makes[130] very little more than five hundred pounds from it. To[140] earn that five hundred pounds countless hours of work have[150] been involved. First of all, the story has had to[160] be invented. Then has come the long task of writing[170] a first draft, and later the typing of the revised[180] copy.

Then a publisher has to be found. A first[190] novel is generally sent to many different publishers before it[200] is accepted. At last the book is published, and reviews[210] of it may appear in the newspapers and magazines. If[220] they are favourable there is a chance that a reasonable[230] amount of money may be earned from the book, but[240] if the reviews are unfavourable the outlook is not good.[250] There is the further fact that Income Tax has to[260] be paid on any money received from royalties, so that[270] the net sum of money in the writer's hands may[280] be quite small.

It is not surprising, therefore, that writers[290] do not like free public libraries. The public library is[300] greatly appreciated by readers who do not want to buy[310] books. There are many reasons why people may not wish[320] to buy books. In the first place, they are expensive,[330] and not everyone can afford to buy them. Secondly, books[340] take up space, and the reader may not have room[350] for any more books on his shelves. An author, however,[360] depends for his money on wide sales, and he is[370] not happy when he receives a royalty on only one[380] copy which may have been read by a hundred people. (390)

(Pitman Examinations Institute)

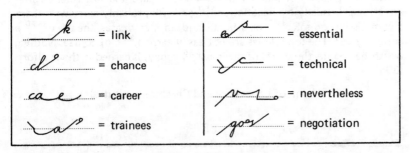

= link	= essential
= chance	= technical
= career	= nevertheless
= trainees	= negotiation

Everything that is made in the world of industry and[10] commerce has to be sold. To sell the products that[20] are manufactured there must be salesmen. If they do not[30] carry out their job efficiently, then the final link in[40] the chain of distribution will suffer. Selling is, therefore, one[50] of the biggest and probably the most intensely competitive businesses[60] in the world today, and it takes a highly-trained[70] person to do it. Such training must leave little to[80] chance and those who make the top grade in the[90] selling market can expect salaries reaching five thousand pounds a[100] year. This is sufficient inducement to the bright young man[110] to make selling his career.

In many cases firms recruit[120] their selling staff from their existing employees. Others accept trainees,[130] selecting them from applicants with a reasonably high standard of[140] general education and the right personality. In the early stages[150] of their career the trainees will spend approximately a year[160] learning how the product is manufactured, the sales and marketing[170] organization within the firm and becoming familiar with the future[180] programme of the company. Trainees are given every encouragement to[190] attend the courses offered by technical colleges on a part-time[200] day or evening basis. Probably the main essential of[210] a good salesman is confidence in the product he is[220] selling and in his own ability to convince the customer.[230] He will know, too, that every time he approaches a[240] possible client he is presenting both the impression of himself[250] and of the firm he is representing. In many cases,[260] he will be dealing with a potential buyer who is[270] a hard-headed business man, who wants to know whether[280] the product one is offering will result in sales.

The[290] salesman who has finished his training is nevertheless always learning[300] and always adding to his experience. This can be done[310] by moving from firm to firm or by remaining with[320] one firm in the hope of progressing up the ladder[330] of promotion.

On the question of salaries, there is no[340] hard and fast rule. Salaries are arranged usually by negotiation[350] and will probably carry with them a commission on sales[360] or a bonus and, in many cases, the use of[370] a company car. The top salaries are not easily earned,[380] of course. Nothing worth having, in the world of business[390] today, is earned without effort. (395)

(Union of Lancashire and Cheshire Institutes)

85

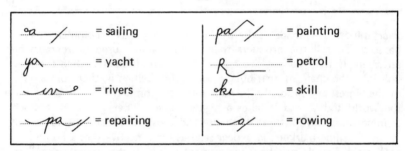

= sailing	= painting
= yacht	= petrol
= rivers	= skill
= repairing	= rowing

In recent years sailing has become a very popular sport.[10] It is a sport that can be enjoyed without having[20] to spend a great deal of money. Of course, if[30] a man buys a very large sailing yacht it is[40] expensive to run and to keep in good condition. However,[50] the small boats that one sees at summer weekends on[60] the rivers and in the quiet waters along our coasts[70] are not expensive. They provide healthy enjoyment in the summer,[80] while in the winter happy hours can be spent repairing[90] sails and painting up the boat ready for the spring.[100]

Motor boats are less popular, and this is no doubt[110] because petrol and oil have to be bought for the[120] engine and much more upkeep is needed. There is also[130] the important fact that if a man has been driving[140] a car all the week he may be very glad[150] to get away from engines and fumes and to enjoy[160] the peace and quiet of the sailing boat. It must[170] be added, however, that in rough weather a sailing boat[180] can be far from peaceful, and considerable skill is needed[190] to handle it well. On smooth inland waters, nevertheless, sailing[200] is indeed a pastime that can be enjoyed by many.[210]

Of course, one advantage of the motor vessel is that[220] it moves much faster, so that one can travel farther[230] in the few leisure hours that may be available. In[240] this way it is possible to enjoy more scenery and[250] perhaps see greater stretches of the river or more creeks[260] and bays around the coast.

Then there are some people[270] who like the rowing boat. Rowing is an excellent form[280] of exercise, but of course is a slow means of[290] transport.

Whatever style of water travel is preferred it is[300] doubtful whether any experience can be more satisfying than to[310] tie up the boat at dusk and to look at[320] the colours thrown on the water by the setting sun.[330]

The increasing interest in water travel in recent years has[340] resulted in the publication of a monthly magazine devoted entirely[350] to this hobby. Not only does it contain interesting stories[360] and the experiences of those who spend their spare time[370] on the water, but it also gives useful hints which[380] boat owners welcome.

It is expected that in the near[390] future more and more people will take up this exercise. (400)

(Pitman Examinations Institute)

86

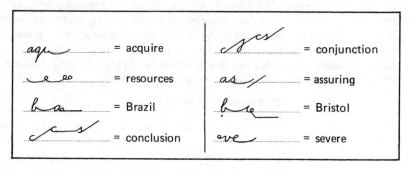

= acquire	= conjunction
= resources	= assuring
= Brazil	= Bristol
= conclusion	= severe

The following is an extract from the Chairman's statement sent[10] out with the Report and Accounts for the year ending[20] 30th June:

"The Group's aim can be pursued in a[30] variety of ways. To follow the direct method is to[40] endeavour to establish or acquire a business with a strong[50] base overseas which can both operate in the local market[60] and also expand its operations both at home and abroad.[70] Our particular commodity has, after investigation, been judged by a[80] specially appointed committee to be a product to which our[90] skills and years of experience can be readily adapted. It[100] is also one in which our resources can be put[110] to profitable use. You will no doubt have realized that[120] this course of action will lend itself to the direct[130] method of development already referred to. Plans have already been[140] developed for major advances in this particular range of products.[150] Such plans will call for further investment, and this must[160] take time to bear fruit and produce results in terms[170] of increased earnings. In order to make a swift rate[180] of progress in this industry your Board decided to make[190] offers for the Share Capital of a long-established company[200] in Brazil. Although the proceedings were somewhat prolonged, they were[210] brought to a satisfactory conclusion on Friday last. The Directors[220] of that Company then agreed to recommend acceptance of our[230] offers, thus assuring us of immediate control. The Group has[240] a large export business and includes subsidiary companies in a[250] number of countries where we also operate. I am happy[260] to say that Mr. Robert Brown has agreed to remain[270] as Chairman and we look forward to the further development[280] of the Company in conjunction with the Board of Directors[290] and the staff.

In the field of packaging your Company[300] maintained its trading profit despite heavy expenditure on development, the[310] costs of running the new plant in Bristol, together with[320] severe competition. During the first six months of the present[330] financial year the trading profit showed an increase, but recent[340] Government measures are beginning to have their effect. It is[350] expected, however, that the trading profit for the whole of[360] the current financial year will show a satisfactory increase over[370] that for last year. In the face of present trading[380] conditions and the amount of development which is now taking place,[390] this can be considered a more than satisfactory achievement." (400)

(Pitman Examinations Institute)

87

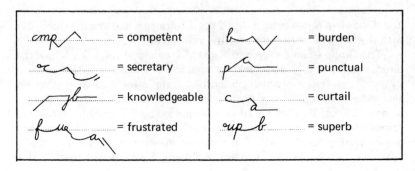

= competent	= burden
= secretary	= punctual
= knowledgeable	= curtail
= frustrated	= superb

A competent secretary is a necessary asset to any business[10] concern, large or small, and the services performed by an[20] efficient secretary are invaluable.

If she is well trained, mature[30] in mind and outlook, intelligent and, above all, knowledgeable about[40] the affairs of the company for which she is working;[50] if she is well groomed, speaks good English and perhaps[60] another language and has a pleasant manner then she is[70] on the way to success. An ability to receive an[80] important client or a fellow business colleague in a correct[90] and pleasant manner is an asset, as is the ability[100] to deal with telephone messages, or any frustrated callers. An[110] efficient secretary must remain calm at all times, must not[120] allow herself to become irritated and, at the same time,[130] she must maintain a sense of humour. A good secretary[140] must remember that it is her first duty to help[150] her employer in any way she can, no matter how[160] small this may seem to be. She is employed to[170] ease the burden and to be relied upon at all[180] times. She must be punctual, devoted to her work and[190] loyal to her firm. She must know what to say[200] under any given circumstances, how to say it and when[210] to say it.

The perfect secretary must be willing to[220] work irregular hours and be pleasantly prepared to curtail her[230] lunch hour. She must be competent in every field of[240] her work and be prepared to make decisions on behalf[250] of her superior as well as be able to interview[260] prospective junior employees. In fact she must be a[270] "Jack-of-all-Trades."

For such a position of importance there[280] is the obvious need for high qualifications, sound common sense,[290] and a keen interest in the work. Many girls attend[300] a secretarial college hoping, eventually, to become a "secretary"[310] but very few actually progress to the top grade, chiefly[320] because they are not prepared to devote the necessary time to[330] study or to work hard.

Top secretaries are a type[340] of career girl, because such work is their life and[350] their whole existence is centred around this. The work is[360] demanding but the rewards are great. Salaries are high; they[370] have the opportunity to travel and their working conditions are[380] superb. For these obvious reasons it is surprising, therefore, that[390] so few girls really endeavour to become the perfect secretary. (400)

(Welsh Joint Education Committee)

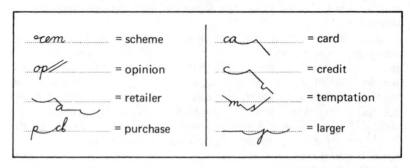

rem	= scheme	*ca*	= card
op	= opinion	*c*	= credit
	= retailer	*m*	= temptation
p ch	= purchase		= larger

In recent years a new scheme has been put into[10] use to help people to do their shopping without using[20] any money. This scheme is organized by some of the[30] banks and is called buying by credit card. It is[40] possible for anyone to apply for a card, and there[50] is no need to have an account with a particular[60] bank. If the person who applies is, in the opinion[70] of the bank, in a position to have credit, then[80] a card is issued to him, and he will be[90] given a note of the sum of money which he[100] will be allowed to owe. Anyone who holds a card[110] may use it to buy goods or services, up to[120] the figure that has been stated, from any of the[130] retailers who show the badge of the bank which has[140] issued the card. At the end of each month, the[150] account has to be settled with the bank. The retailers[160] who wish to show the badge have to pay a[170] fee of five pounds to join, and on each purchase[180] which is made by a customer who holds a card,[190] he pays a small service charge. The bank then settles[200] up all the accounts with him.

This system has advantages[210] both for the customer and for the retailer. The customer[220] can have goods to a set amount on credit. Also[230] he can use a small card to pay bills in[240] a variety of places, such as shops, planes and hotels,[250] without having to carry large sums of money with him.[260] From the point of view of the retailer, the bank[270] or organization which issues the credit card gives a guarantee[280] that payment will be made, and this reduces his bad[290] debts. He can also reduce the amount of working capital[300] required for the business, and his turnover may be increased[310] because he offers this service. Those who run credit card[320] schemes can make their profit from the service charges.

It[330] has been said that those who use the cards may[340] find that prices rise, as service charges will be passed[350] on to them. In addition, there will always be the[360] temptation to run up accounts that are larger than they[370] would be if payment were made in cash. In spite[380] of these things, however, it seems likely that the use[390] of credit cards will increase in the next few years. (400)

(London Chamber of Commerce)

89

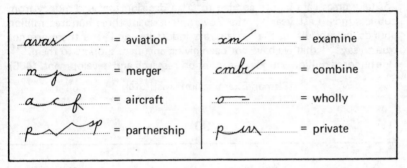

avas	= aviation	*xm*	= examine
m j	= merger	*cmbr*	= combine
a c f	= aircraft	*o*	= wholly
p sp	= partnership	*p m*	= private

The Minister for Aviation said: The Government is very pleased[10] to learn of the merger between these two great aircraft[20] companies, and hopes that a further one will be announced[30] in the very near future. In these days it is[40] not desirable to leave these matters to chance, because the[50] aircraft industry is so very important to the country. It[60] has vast commitments both at home and abroad. The Government[70] therefore is considering the advantages of taking part in the[80] management of the industry. When this matter is under consideration[90] it must be remembered that the Government has already provided[100] a large part of the working capital of the undertakings,[110] and has helped to make important decisions on new projects.[120] It is to be hoped that any partnership that may[130] take place between the Government and the aircraft industry will[140] be on a mutually agreed basis. The Government has therefore[150] come to the conclusion that the national interest will be[160] best served if the remaining two large aircraft companies are[170] merged into one, in which the Government would take[180] a large interest. These companies have said that in the[190] circumstances they are willing to co-operate with the Government.[200] They will examine in detail what is the best means[210] of achieving satisfaction for everyone who would be affected by[220] the changes. The aim of a merger is to combine[230] resources and labour in such a way that the maximum[240] use is made of them.

Two major problems face the[250] aircraft industry today. The first is to achieve one hundred[260] per cent efficiency, and the second is to build up[270] as much competitive ability as possible. The industry must be[280] able to produce the right kind of plane at the[290] right time. The plane must also be produced at the[300] right cost. This has been important while the industry has[310] been wholly private, but it will become still more important[320] when the Government has a share in its activities. The[330] Government would be failing in its duty to the public[340] if it did not take great care before coming to[350] a decision to spend money from public funds. Last year[360] the Government spent three hundred million pounds in subsidizing the[370] aircraft industries, and it is therefore not true to say[380] that we have not been giving adequate support to them.[390] One hundred million pounds was spent on research and development. (400)

(Pitman Examinations Institute)

90

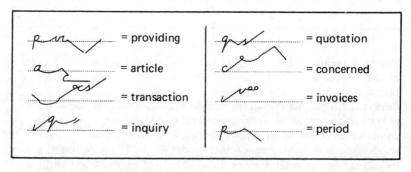

The purpose of all businesses is to make a profit.[10] The profit comes from the difference between the cost price[20] and the selling price of the articles which are sold,[30] or, in the case of businesses which provide services, it[40] comes from the difference between the cost of providing the[50] service and the price which the customer pays for it.[60] The whole business of buying and selling an article is[70] known as a transaction. During the course of a transaction[80] a great deal of information has to pass between the[90] buyer and the seller. First of all, an inquiry is[100] sent by the person wishing to make the purchase. This[110] will state the goods required, and the quantity that is[120] needed, and it will probably give a delivery date. In[130] reply to an inquiry, a quotation is sent. This states[140] the goods available, the prices, and the delivery date. A[150] catalogue or price list is

84

often sent with the quotation.[160] When the quotation has been received, the purchaser has to[170] decide which firm is to have the order. He will[180] have to consider the quality, price, and the delivery date[190] that is offered. The order will then be sent to[200] the firm that has been chosen, and will state the[210] goods required, and the quoted price. The purchaser will keep[220] a copy of the order so that he knows what[230] he has ordered.

When the firm has received the order[240] it is usual for copies of it to be given[250] to the different departments which are concerned with it. A[260] dispatch note will be sent to the packing department and[270] sometimes it is then sent to the purchaser so that[280] he knows that the goods are on their way. The[290] top copy of the set is known as the invoice.[300] This lists the goods purchased and tells the purchaser how[310] much he owes for them. When the goods have been[320] received, the purchaser will check them against the invoice to[330] make sure the quantity and quality are what he ordered.[340] A record is kept of all the invoices which are[350] sent to each customer. At the end of each month[360] or each quarter a copy of the amounts is made[370] on a statement of account which tells the purchaser the[380] total sum which he owes for the period. Few firms[390] send receipts as the cheques when paid act as receipts. (400)

(London Chamber of Commerce)

91

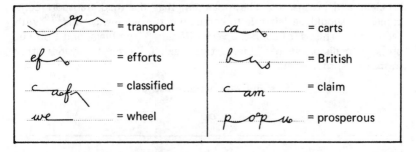

= transport	= carts
= efforts	= British
= classified	= claim
= wheel	= prosperous

Transport plays a very important part in the modern world.[10] I am sure you will fully appreciate the importance of[20] transport if you will just think for a moment about[30] what life would be like if all forms of transport[40] were to disappear and people had to depend on their[60] own efforts to get the goods they wanted.

There are[60] many types of transport but they can all be classified[70] into three main kinds. There is transport by land, by[80] sea, and by air. Let us first consider transport by^{90} land. It was a wonderful day for mankind when someone^{100} made the first wheel. We depend to a very great^{110} extent on the wheel in our day-to-day lives.^{120} The farmer must have carts or trucks to take his^{130} produce to the market. Lorries are required to carry raw^{140} materials to factories, and lorries are, of course, also required^{150} to carry the finished articles from the factories to the^{160} shops. Vans are needed to take articles from the shops^{170} to the customers. You will agree, therefore, that road transport^{180} is of great importance.

Then there is transport by rail.^{190} Although the carriage of goods by road has increased at^{200} a faster rate during recent years, many goods are still^{210} carried for long distances by the railways. In this country^{220} the railway system was considered to be of such basic^{230} importance to the economy that it was taken over by^{240} the State. There are now no private railway companies. Instead^{250} there is a public corporation which is known as British^{260} Rail. In the opinion of many people there should be^{270} a proper division of the business between the railways and^{280} the road transport companies. Some people even go so far^{290} as to express the view that the big road transport^{300} companies should also be made into a public corporation. They^{310} believe that, instead of having competition between the two forms^{320} of transport, it would be better to have co-operation. This^{330} view is not accepted by certain other people who claim^{340} that it is the forces of competition that make organizations^{350} efficient and prosperous. They maintain that the road transport companies^{360} should be left free to compete with the railways and^{370} with each other. This is, of course, a very difficult^{380} problem, and I do not propose to discuss it in^{390} detail this evening. We must consider other forms of transport. (400)

(Pitman Examinations Institute)

92

fa	= fatal	*fa ll*	= farthest
ac	= accidents	*p ob*	= prohibit
e f	= certificates	*a ob*	= advisable
bo	= buoyant	*xp*	= explore

The first fatal bathing accidents of the year have already[10] been reported, and there will without doubt be more. Yet[20] most, if not all of them, could be avoided.

You[30] may be able to swim like a fish, have enough[40] certificates to paper your bedroom wall, and enough gold medals[50] to start your own mint; but this does not mean[60] that you are a hundred per cent proof against getting[70] into difficulties.

Of course there are dangers. You may find[80] that you are able to swim better in the sea:[90] salt water is far more buoyant than the clear water[100] of your local swimming pool, but do not be tempted[110] to think that you can swim farther. Remember that once[120] out of your depth, tired and aching, you cannot just[130] swim to the side and climb out.

Do not be[140] swayed by "dares" to prove yourself. If you want to[150] show everyone how far you can swim, do it within[160] your depth rather than aiming to reach the farthest swimmer[170] at sea.

If you fail to catch that new beach[180] ball, and it goes flying past you away out to[190] sea, do not swim out in hot pursuit because you[200] are afraid to lose face in front of your friends.[210] The odds are that they would not attempt it!

Do[220] not ignore signs which prohibit swimming beyond a certain boundary,[230] even if you can see no apparent reason for them.[240] They are usually there to protect you from fast tides and[250] currents which are dangerous.

If you are still in[260] the sinking stages, and still striking bottom, keep a close[270] watch on the tide. Swim when the tide is mid-way[280] in, when the wind is light, and there are not[290] too many waves.

Time your swim so that it is[300] not too close to a meal. It is not advisable[310] to swim until at least an hour after eating, as[320] this can cause severe cramp.

Even if you are not[330] too confident about your own unaided efforts, and a little[340] bit doubtful about "going it alone," it is just[350] as well not to place too much trust in such[360] things as rubber tyres. They may let you down; and[370] be especially wary when the tide is on the turn.[380]

There may be small islands or rocks which you are[390] tempted to explore; but be sure that the tide is[400] on the way out or you are likely to be[410] stranded. Above all, be aware always of your own limitations. (420)

(Royal Society of Arts)

cab (shorthand)	= cabinets	*(shorthand)*	= correspondence
(shorthand)	= problem	*(shorthand)*	= library
(shorthand)	= dispose	*(shorthand)*	= confidential
(shorthand)	= acknowledgments	*(shorthand)*	= accessible

There are many good reasons why the mass of paper[10] that is kept in the office should be cut down[20] as much as possible. The actual space taken by the[30] office costs a great deal of money, and filing cabinets[40] also are expensive and take up valuable space. Then someone[50] has to be paid to keep the files in order[60] and up to date. There is a considerable fire risk[70] in keeping large quantities of paper and, lastly, the more[80] pieces of paper there are in the office, the more[90] difficult it is to find any one particular piece. But,[100] even if one accepts the fact that a lot of[110] unnecessary paper is stored in many offices, there still remains[120] the problem of what to throw away and of how[130] and when to dispose of it.

There are, of course,[140] some documents that need never be put in a file.[150] Letters which are simply acknowledgments do not have to be[160] kept and some other letters need to be filed only[170] until a reply is received. Apart from correspondence, some material[180] is kept for information only, such as books of reference,[190] magazines and newspapers. Books of reference that are up to[200] date are essential in any office, but it is not[210] always worth keeping old editions of them, or back numbers[220] of magazines in case they are needed. The test is[230] to ask how easily the information may be found from[240] other sources. If there is a reference library within an[250] easy distance and it stores back numbers of the same[260] magazine, and if they are needed only occasionally, there is[270] not much point in keeping them.

The most usual way[280] of getting rid of waste paper is to throw it[290] into the wastepaper basket, or send it in a sack[300] to be made into pulp. Material that is confidential should[310] never be treated in this way but the paper should[320] be torn into pieces so small that it is impossible[330] for anyone to read it. In some offices a machine[340] is kept for this purpose. For material that has to[350] be kept for a certain length of time but is[360] not often needed for reference, transfer files may be used,[370] and these can be stored in a less accessible place.[380] It is important, however, to make sure that a note[390] is put on the current file of what material has[400] been placed in a transfer file.

Rules about when a[410] document may be destroyed must be devised, and everyone who[420] works on the filing system must know them. Generally, the[430] only problem is to work out a system that makes[440] it quite clear when a document is no longer useful. (450)

(London Chamber of Commerce)

94

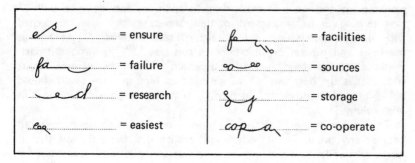

= ensure	= facilities
= failure	= sources
= research	= storage
= easiest	= co-operate

There was a time when the people who were in[10] charge of sales departments were of the opinion that they[20] could sell anything and everything. When an article did not[30] sell well, the reason was thought to be that the[40] price was too high. But, at the present time, selling[50] in itself is not enough to ensure success: the whole[60] business has to be one of very carefully planned marketing.[70]

Marketing, of course, means a great deal more than selling.[80] In fact, the success or failure of the business as[90] a whole depends on the way the marketing is done.[100] One of the reasons for this is that now machines[110] can deal with facts and information, and many things can[120] be worked out which would take so long to do[130] without machines that the answers would never be up to[140] date. If marketing is carried out successfully, the customer will[150] get what he wants when he wants it, at the[160] price which he is willing to pay, and the manufacturer[170] or supplier will get a fair profit in return for[180] his services.

The first need is for careful market research[190] in order to find out what it is that the[200] customer thinks he wants rather than what the manufacturer thinks[210] he ought to have because that is what he is[220] best at making. Then the quantity of goods needed and[230] the time when they are wanted must be discovered. Research[240] must find how the customer likes the goods packed, which[250] is not necessarily how the factory finds it easiest to[260] pack them, and how much the customer is prepared to[270] pay. If these inquiries are carried out with care, the[280] mass of facts and information, when put together, will show[290] the business firm what its aims should be.

When it[300] is known what the customer wants, it is possible to[310] work out what facilities are required to give it to[320] him. Facilities, of course, will include machinery and the men[330] who are needed to work it as well as the[340] type of materials and sources of supply and methods of[350] production. It will be necessary also to look into problems[360] of management and ways of marketing. In addition, consideration will[370] have to be given to departments of the business which[380] are concerned with finance, purchasing and storage of raw materials[390] as well as transport and general organization. In this way,[400] the various departments can co-operate in an effort to ascertain[410] what the customer wants and what is the best way[420] of giving it to him, and the result should be[430] a great improvement in profits, as well as a great[440] increase in sales volume.

This means the end of the[450] time when sales departments wanted sales at any price. The[460] sales staff realize that the only sale that is worth[470] while is the one that produces a profit. The successful[480] businesses are those which can find the answers to their faults[490] and come nearest to filling the needs of their[500] customers. (501)

(London Chamber of Commerce)

95

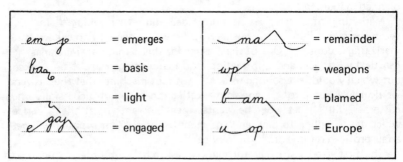

= emerges			= remainder
= basis			= weapons
= light			= blamed
= engaged			= Europe

One of the principal points that emerges from the report[10] is that Great Britain really needs an aircraft industry which[20] is smaller but stronger.

One of the major difficulties that[30] Britain has to face is that the home market for[40] aircraft is small, whereas the industry requires to operate on[50] a very large scale if it is to be successful[60] from a financial point of view. This difficulty must be[70] accepted as a basis for future policy if the industry[80] is to be put on to a satisfactory footing.

In[90] the light of these remarks it is interesting to examine[100] the present position of the industry. At present there are[110] more than three hundred factories concerned in the manufacture of[120] aircraft, and these factories together employ over a quarter of[130] a million workers. Of these quarter of a million workers[140] about forty per cent are engaged on the production of[150] frames and thirty per cent on the production of engines.[160] Of the remaining thirty per cent we find that about[170] one half are employed on the equipment that is used[180] in planes, and the remainder on guided weapons. The value[190] of the output of these factories remains fairly steady, and[200] is about five hundred million pounds annually. Only twenty-five[210] per cent of the output is at present exported.

The[220] report on the industry states that during the years 1949[230] to 1956[240] it expanded at a satisfactory rate but thereafter its record[250] has been very disappointing. This is partly blamed upon the[260] policy of successive governments. The British government has seemed unable[270] to make up its mind to follow a consistent policy.[280] There have been many delays in making decisions, and, still[290] worse, there have been changes of policy when projects have[300] already been commenced. As a result, it has sometimes been[310] found necessary to abandon work after a great deal of[320] money has been spent. This is largely because there has[330] not been sufficient research into the value of a new[340] aircraft before work on it has been begun. So far[350] as exports are concerned, the report considers that the government,[360] as well as the industry, has made inadequate attempts to[370] secure orders from overseas. When such orders have been secured,[380] the manufacturers have very often failed to meet the delivery[390] dates promised. There was some re-organization of the industry in[400] 1960, but the completion of this merger[410] has been slow and is not fully realized even today.[420] One of the most important recommendations of the committee is[430] that the aircraft industry shall do everything in its power[440] to extend its markets. It also makes the recommendation that[450] the industry shall share development costs through encouraging international co-operation.[460] Such a policy should be pursued with a clear sense[470] of direction. As other countries in Europe suffer from much[480] the same troubles as Great Britain in this respect, it[490] should not be difficult to open negotiations for such collaboration. (500)

(Pitman Examinations Institute)

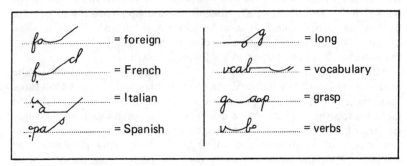

= foreign			= long
= French			= vocabulary
= Italian			= grasp
= Spanish			= verbs

Many people learn a foreign language at school. For the[10] English school child the first foreign language to be learnt[20] is generally French. If a second language is then mastered[30] it may be German or Italian, or perhaps Spanish. For[40] many children in countries spread throughout the world the first[50] foreign language that they learn is English. We therefore have[60] the position that hundreds of thousands of children every year[70] spend a considerable amount of time studying a language other[80] than their own. This is a very good thing, but[90] the great pity is that when the children leave school[100] they seldom use that language any more. Unless they take[110] up employment which demands the use of a foreign language[120] they generally put away their books, and in a short[130] time remember little or nothing of what they have learnt.[140]

What a great waste of time and effort this is![150] It is not always possible for students to visit the[160] countries where the language they have learnt is spoken, but[170] it is easily possible for them to read books written[180] in that tongue. Two obvious advantages would be derived from[190] such reading. In the first place, the students' vocabulary would[200] increase, and the idioms and expressions used by the people[210] would become familiar. In the second place, the range of[220] reading available to the students would be greatly widened. Novels,[230] poems, and even technical books could be read in the[240] foreign language, and such reading would bring much interest. A[250] novel which might not be sufficiently important to interest a[260] person if read in his own language can seem very[270] delightful indeed when read in a language which is not[280] his own. Through such reading an insight can be gained[290] into the ways of life in other countries. Even the[300] countryside can become familiar, although the reader has not actually[310] visited it.

When a student has fallen into the habit[320] of reading books in one foreign language he will probably[330] be sufficiently interested to learn a second one. Here it is[340] important to emphasize that for the purposes of reading[350] one's grasp of a language does not have to be[360] as good as it does for purposes of speech. When[370] speaking a foreign language the rules of grammar must be[380] observed, and tenses used correctly. When reading, however, correct grammar[390] and the proper use of verbs is already there, and[400] only an accurate translation has to be achieved. This is,[410] indeed, a highly important difference, as it means that a[420] person who is interested in literature or in some special[430] technical subject can read books written in a foreign language[440] although their knowledge of the language is not great. It[450] is not at all uncommon to find people who read[460] with equal facility in three or four different languages. Such[470] people find the variation in tongue and style stimulating, and[480] they would feel very restricted if they suddenly found themselves[490] forced to read books written only in their mother tongue. (500)

(Pitman Examinations Institute)

97

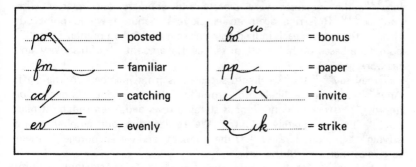

̴̴̴̴̴	= posted	̴̴̴̴̴	= bonus
̴̴̴̴̴	= familiar	̴̴̴̴̴	= paper
̴̴̴̴̴	= catching	̴̴̴̴̴	= invite
̴̴̴̴̴	= evenly	̴̴̴̴̴	= strike

As the directors' report and accounts were posted to you[10] two weeks ago, I assume you are all familiar with[20] their contents. You will see that the progress made by[30] the company during the last few years has been maintained.[40] Our trade has continued to improve steadily. We have sold[50] more goods than ever before. The prices of some things[60] have again risen, but others have remained stable, and a[70] few articles have actually fallen in price. It is possible[80] therefore that we have already reached the peak in prices[90] and that further falls may be expected. In some lines[100] production is catching up with demand.

You will see the[110] directors recommend the payment of a final dividend of five[120] per cent, so that the total distribution for the year[130] is ten per cent, which is the same as last^{140} year. In recent years our policy has been to try^{150} to ensure sufficient cash balances to meet the ordinary claims^{160} of the business, plus a margin for any extra expenses^{170} that might occur.

At the end of the year, repairs^{180} to our various properties were very much in arrear. The^{190} cost of these repairs has been spread as evenly as^{200} possible over the years, and we are gradually overtaking the^{210} arrears.

The profit sharing scheme, started last year for the^{220} benefit of our employees, promises to be a success. The^{230} members of our staff are encouraged to become shareholders in^{240} the company. Besides that, everyone with at least twelve months'^{250} service receives a bonus, if the profits permit it. The^{260} total amount of the bonus depends upon the net profit^{270} for the year. The purpose of relating bonus to net^{280} profit is to encourage the members of the staff to^{290} assist the directors in trying to save expenses. Some expenses^{300} we cannot do much about, because they are outside our^{310} control, but this does not apply to such items as^{320} lighting, paper, and delivery charges. The directors themselves look into^{330} the expenses very closely and compare one quarter with another.^{340} Referring again to employees' bonus, I would point out that^{350} the amount each individual receives is decided on points. These^{360} points are based on his length of service, the amount^{370} of his salary, and his work generally.

I may say^{380} that we invite suggestions from members of the staff. Any^{390} suggestion likely to promote sales or reduce expenses or improve^{400} working conditions is suitably rewarded, even though it may not^{410} be immediately adopted. We realize that our employees are serving^{420} the public as well as the company, and we encourage^{430} them to give of their best all the time.

Prospects^{440} for the future are good. There is considerable activity in^{450} our trade, and we do not expect any labour troubles.^{460} The policy I have just referred to with regard to^{470} our employees promotes good feeling, and we have never had^{480} a strike. I look forward to seeing you next year^{490} with as good news as I have given you today. (500)

(Pitman Examinations Institute)

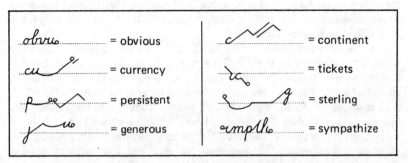

obrus	= obvious	*continent*	= continent
cu	= currency	*tickets*	= tickets
p	= persistent	*sterling*	= sterling
generous	= generous	*sympthe*	= sympathize

The Right Hon. Gentleman said: I wish to give my[10] full support to the Hon. Member who has just spoken.[20] It must be obvious to every clear-thinking person that[30] the Government is right in taking this serious step. This[40] country cannot afford to continue the practice of allowing an[50] unlimited number of people large sums of foreign currency to[60] spend on holidays abroad.

Naturally, this is a matter for[70] considerable regret because, as a nation, we like to be[80] free and to place as few restrictions as possible upon[90] the liberties of the people. The persistent adverse balance of[100] payments makes it impossible for the Government at the present[110] time to maintain a policy of generous travel allowances for[120] holidays on the Continent and elsewhere outside the sterling area.[130] It is admitted that the amount of £50 is[140] not very much in these days of high costs, and[150] it is inevitable that many people who were looking forward[160] to travelling on the Continent or visiting the United States[170] of America in the near future will not be able[180] to do so. On the other hand, if the method[190] of travel is wisely chosen holiday-makers will be surprised[200] to find how far that £50 can be made[210] to stretch.

For instance, all journeys should be made through[220] British companies as far as this is practicable. Journeys by[230] air can be made to all parts of the world[240] on British-owned planes, and the tickets can be paid[250] for in sterling. The same is true of our ships.[260] It is possible to travel thousands of miles by ship,[270] paying for the trip in sterling. The only foreign currency[280] which need be used is that required for visits ashore[290] in places outside the sterling area. Fortunately, the various shipping[300] companies and air lines are showing themselves fully aware of[310] the advantages that they now have, and are advertising widely.[320]

Another form of holiday which provides wonderful opportunities for pleasure[330] and relaxation but which demands very little in the way[340] of foreign currency is the cruise by sea. Many very[350] attractive cruises are now being offered, and only today[360] I read an advertisement offering a two weeks cruise, visiting various[370] islands in the sun and costing from only £70[380] upwards, inclusive.

On the whole, therefore, I do not find[390] it easy to sympathize with those who claim that the[400] Government is making it impossible for English people to visit[410] other countries. Those who are determined to visit countries which[420] are not in the sterling area will still find that[430] it is possible to do so, although they cannot hope[440] to have unlimited money to spend when they arrive. Others[450] will perhaps be surprised to to find what pleasant holidays can[460] be spent in their own country.

It is therefore my[470] intention to give my full support to the Government measure.[480] I hope all Members of this House will share my[490] intention, and act in the best interests of the country. (500)

(Pitman Examinations Institute)

99

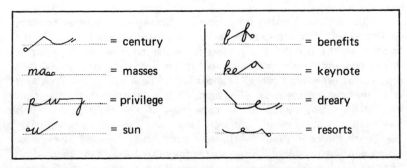

	= century		= benefits
	= masses		= keynote
	= privilege		= dreary
	= sun		= resorts

Holidays with pay are an accepted part of our lives.[10] It is certainly not easy for us to realize that[20] at the beginning of this century great numbers of the[30] workers of this country did not receive pay during a[40] holiday period. If they wanted to go away for a[50] holiday it was necessary for them not only to save[60] for the holiday itself but to save also to make[70] up for the loss of pay while they were not[80] attending work. Conditions for the masses of the workers have[90] steadily improved as the years have passed, and one great[100] privilege now shared by almost all workers is that of[110] receiving full payment while enjoying a vacation.

Today twenty[120] or thirty million people leave their homes and go away for[130] a holiday in the summer. Some go far afield. They[140] seek the sun, and are willing to pay high transport[150] costs to find it. The additional cost of a holiday[160] abroad is not caused, as a rule, through hotels or[170] boarding houses being more expensive. High transport charges are the[180] usual reason for holidays in sunny places overseas costing more[190] than an equal length of time spent at a local[200] seaside resort. Many families cut the transport costs by travelling[210] in their own car. This undoubtedly saves money, but it[220] is open to question whether a man benefits much from[230] his holiday if he is forced to drive his car[240] for long distances on busy and over-crowded roads. He[250] certainly cannot relax while driving, and relaxation should be the[260] keynote of a holiday. On the other hand, many drivers[270] state that they much prefer to drive their own cars[280] because it gives them the opportunity to stop where and[290] when they wish. This is very true. Those who travel[300] by air rarely see very much except the rather dreary[310] airports. In these days aeroplanes fly at great heights above[320] the clouds, and the air traveller looks out upon a[330] white world, which is beautiful but monotonous. Below the clouds[340] there is an ever-changing scene, but unfortunately he cannot[350] see it.

The holiday-maker who travels by train has[360] a better chance to see the countryside. A train is[370] a most pleasant means of transport, except during very busy[380] times, and it is strange that it is not more[390] popular. In a train it is possible to sit in[400] armchair comfort, order meals, and watch the fields, hills, and[410] villages. No effort has to be made to obtain enjoyment.[420] It is there for the taking.

Not everyone goes far[430] away for a holiday, however. Millions of people are satisfied[440] to visit our own coast resorts, where many amusements are[450] readily available. Many kinds of accommodation can be found, varying[460] from the large and expensive hotel to the small but[470] cheaper boarding house. There are beautiful sandy beaches, on which[480] to sun-bathe or play, and there are pleasant downs[490] which may be climbed if the holiday-maker feels energetic.[500]

Thousands of other people just stay at home. The man[510] of the house probably does odd jobs that have been[520] waiting months for his attention. Unfortunately, although this kind of[530] holiday is a change for the man it offers little[540] in the way of change and rest for his wife. (550)

(Pitman Examinations Institute)

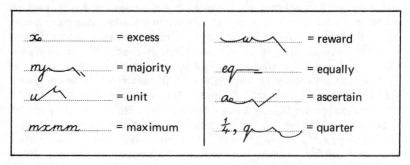

In the course of his remarks the Chairman said: This[10] year it is again my pleasant duty to inform you[20] of the record results of your company. I draw your[30] attention to the Accounts, from which you will see that[40] the trading profits for the year under review were in[50] excess of one and a half million pounds. I am[60] very proud of this achievement, for it represents an increase[70] of almost fifteen per cent in the trading profits at[80] a time when trading conditions were at their worst for[90] the majority of companies. You will also notice from the[100] Accounts that the turnover was greatly increased, but I must[110] point out that our increase in profits was to a[120] large extent the result of a decrease in the cost[130] per unit of production.

You will be interested to learn[140] that our increased production was brought about with a reduced[150] labour force. In fact, we employed some five per cent[160] less people in the year under review than we employed[170] in the previous year. I think you will all agree[180] with me when I say that this is proof of[190] our methods of obtaining the maximum efficiency. One of these[200] methods, which I say is in actual fact probably the[210] most important, is to pay all our productive labour according[220] to results. The greater the productivity the greater will be[230] the reward. We do much more than this, however, for[240] we ensure that the latest equipment is used by our[250] workers.

It has long been the practice for the sales[260] staff to receive most of their reward in the form[270] of commission. The more they sell the more they earn[280] for themselves. The best salesmen cannot get good results if[290] they are trying to sell a bad product. We are[300] making sure that our workers produce the very best articles[310] possible. Not only do they use the most up-to-[320] date machines, but they have the help of the latest[330] testing equipment. When our customers buy our products they are[340] certain to get goods of the highest quality. This is[350] because our research department goes to a lot of trouble[360] to find out all the various needs of the different[370] markets.

Because of our ability to produce the best articles[380] at the lowest possible cost, our goods are sold in[390] the face of competition in most countries of the world.[400] You may be interested to know the chief markets we[410] supply in addition to that of this country. One quarter[420] of the total export is sold to the United States.[430] One fifth is exported to South Africa, and the balance[440] is shared equally between Europe and Australia. In the current[450] year our exports increased by ten per cent, and we[460] continue to do all we can to sell more of[470] our products in foreign markets.

You will be pleased to[480] learn that in the first quarter of this year our[490] sales were at a higher rate than for the corresponding[500] period of last year. In view of these results, it[510] would have been reasonable for the dividend for the year[520] to have been increased to twenty-five per cent. Owing[530] to the present policy of the Government, this is not[540] now possible and the dividend remains at twenty per cent. (550)

(Pitman Examinations Institute)